Sea Marks

by Gardner McKay

A Samuel French Acting Edition

SAMUELFRENCH.COM

ISBN 978-0-573-61881-9 Printed in U.S.A. #21053

"Sea Marks" is dedicated to its first cast; Judith Roberts and Joshua Bryant; Evergreen Stage and Actors Studio West productions, 1971. And to Walter Kerr who, much later, in 1981, did what a critic does best.

PLAYERS THEATRE

DANA MATTHOW and DEBORAH MATTHOW
present

by Gardner McKay

starring

JOHN GETZ *LESLIE LYLES*

costumes by
RICHARD HORNUNG

scenery by
LESLIE TAYLOR & DALE JORDAN

lighting by
TODD ELMER

production stage manager
TOM W. PICARD

directed by

John Stix

THE PERSONS IN THE PLAY:

COLM PRIMROSE—An Irish fisherman from the western islands.

TIMOTHEA STILES—A lady, not much younger than Colm, who was once from Wales.

TIME: The recent past.

PLACE: Cliffhorn Heads, an island in the west of Ireland; a cottage there, a graveyard.
And Liverpool; a flat, a ladies club.

(Colm may be played between the ages of 35 and 65. Timothea's age should rise in proportion to his.)

IMPORTANT ADVERTISING NOTE

The following credit line must be given on all programs:

Originally Produced Off-Broadway by Dana Matthow and Deborah Matthow

Colm's island: **The Heads is a curious place—an uncomplicated** society—but it exists, not by this name, but by other names and in other parts of the world. The Heads is a dying island, like certain other western islands; the world is changing and the Heads is unable to change. The younger generations have gone out into the world and stayed. The turf (fuel) dug on the island is harder to come by. Even the fish they kill are being stolen by large trawlers under different flags that slip into their waters. The men here have an inherited quality of gloom about them (fundamentally, since Cromwell's invasion) but, as well, there is an unspoken "better-news-tomorrow" attitude that goes with a crank of the head and the morning greeting. It is a cheerfulness based on ancient setbacks rather than the current ones.

The men here are not tall and they are lean; there's no man with anything on his body but the wire he needs to row and haul. A fat man seen on these islands is either a priest or a relative from America. This is no choice-softened society. Still, it exists; without telephone, television, or airstrip. Whatever comes on or goes off the island comes through the surf and crosses the beach. The one lightbulb on the island hangs in the licensed public drinking house (the Captain's) run by a man and wife who keep their generator running a few hours each evening. There are no cars on the island; no roads. There are many high-walled lanes (boreens) made of stones cleared from the land and they give shelter to walkers from the wind.

Colm lives on an island, like so many of us, and his mood is made of what there is for him to look forward to. His history is of little interest here, even as subtext, but his name might be of significance to whoever might be using it. No last names are used on this small island and fathers are designated from their sons by their middle names. Primrose (prime-rose: first flower) was given him (because of his springtime birthing) by a man who had loved his mother. This man—The MacAfee—raised Colm after she was drowned by a wave that sucked her off a rock while she was doing her wash—at Cliffhorn Heads.

—Gardner McKay

Sea Marks

ACT ONE

SCENE 1

The stage is black; and, for a time, the audience hears sounds of the sea, the wind and maybe the rain.

When the lights come up, far to one side of the stage, we see the lower room of a stone cottage on one of the western islands in Ireland. It is morning. A strong man is looking through a window, toward the audience, at the weather. He wears heavy wool socks, patched sea-pants (or wool pants) with the suspenders dangling, and an undyed wool sweater, stained to the color of pale tea. On his table is an enamel cup, paper, a pencil, a knife. Close-by is a stove with an iron pot. A yellow oilskin coat and a black sou'wester hang on pegs. Sea boots hang there, too, with a line running through the tops of each. Eventually, he turns away and sits in a carved chair by the table.

He talks to himself, including the audience, summing up the terminal sameness of his life, maybe composing a letter. It is his birthday and he is on the verge of something new.

COLM. I live by the sea.
I have always lived by the sea.
I can't know what it would be like living anywhere else.
The house I live in is made of stone that the sea has broken from these cliffs. It is a small house and stands close to the edge of the full tide. I am watching the sea now. It pushes up on the beach in front of the house. It is not a pretty beach. It is made of gray stones which the sea turns black by rising over them and falling away. The rain has stopped now and the sea is gray. The sky is white and lines of gray are being blown along further out at sea. There is always a gale somewhere on a day like this.
Each morning by the way the sea looks, I know how to feel. Its mood varies and so does mine. I can hear the sea, too, always. And I've seen every kind of fit it's able to throw against this shore. This shore. This shore is all the sea I know. The sea is a continent, and all I know of it are a few miles of this shore.
My house was built before I was born. And it was built away from the sea wall and a mile from the fishing harbor. There is a room upstairs and a room downstairs. It is easy to heat from turf, or if there is wood, wood. I painted it white a few years back because no other house is white and I could better see it from off-shore when I went out to fish. I also painted it white because I felt like it.
I don't very often do things I feel like. Neither does anyone else around here. I know everyone around here and everyone knows me. We were all born on this island, and that's that. But because we began by the sea and have lived by the sea, there is no want to do anything apart from the sea. We could not be closer to the sea without drowning in it, which is what a few of us do every year.

Each spring when we tar the hulls and get ready for the mackerel, we sing some songs, the same songs. And when we're tired of working, we go to the Captain's and drink until wives start appearing at the door. But I have never married and find my way home alone.

I had a dog a few years back, I did, a black dog who went with me everywhere, even to fish. And when he died of fish poisoning, I missed him. Ah, he couldn't cook and he couldn't light the fire, and he was no good to talk to, but I missed him sitting there by the door. I suppose I still do. He cannot be replaced.

Some birds come around, sea birds, and they come up to me to feed. I give them bread or whatever scraps there is. The birds have wingspan, sure, but no sense, no feeling.

The wind blows off the sea. The only time I've ever seen it blow any other way was in the middle of storms when everything is confused and the wind backs around and seems to be coming from inside the cliffs.

I have a lot to remember and, I suppose, something to look forward to. Mainly I remember how lucky I've been, coming off the water at night. And the times I thought I might drown.

But I remember small things, too. There was a wedding where I met this girl from Liverpool, Maggie's cousin, visiting for a week. Pretty girl. Around here you don't see a girl like that.

(*A special light comes up on* TIMOTHEA. *She stands, in coat and scarf, by a mantel at the opposite side of the stage, holding an unopened envelope. She places it on the mantel and stoops to light the gas heater within the fireplace. Her flat is barely seen in the dimness of the spilled light; it is staid, high-ceilinged and dark panneled, factors she has tried to overcome with certain gay touches; bright fabrics and small, framed photographs.*)

COLM. Around here you don't court a girl unless you go to marry that girl. And I have never married. And so I have never courted. There was my teacher, Miss Minott, I think I loved her, but I was so young. You see, it's not a big place, the Heads, and I got to fishing, and that was what I did. I've been to Galway, but I've never paid to lay with a harridan. And so, I've never . . . courted.

(TIMOTHEA *blows out the match, opens the envelope and reads.*)

COLM. I'm looking down at the sea and I have some feeling there from the sea. (*Colm smiles, maybe laughs, and abruptly turns from the window.*) Something like the start of love. (*He takes a chamber pot from his wooden chest.*) It was a pretty girl at the wedding. I talked with her. Would she remember? That was last winter. No, two winters ago.

(*The light on* COLM *fades to black as he turns upstage with the chamber pot.* TIMOTHEA *finishes reading his letter.*)

TIMOTHEA. "And so I know you don't remember me, Miss Stiles, but I was the fellow at the wedding. You might have seen me standing by the beverage bowl looking at you? You *must* remember me because while I was standing looking at you, I leaned my arm to the table to give me an air of easiness and put my hand into the bowl up to the elbow, and then stood there dripping like a net of fish for all to see.

If you didn't take notice of that, you must be a very *kind* person indeed. I talks to the MacAfee about you, and he says you're not married still, so it's alright to send you this letter. But he says you wouldn't remember me either, because, he says, you wouldn't take notice of a plain fisherman. But whether you would or wouldn't, would you be good enough to answer this letter so that I know you got it? It's been cold this year longer than I can remember, but winter's nearly passed away.
Truly yours, Colm Primrose."

(*A month has passed. As the lights fade on* TIMOTHEA, *they come up on* COLM, *in wet sou'wester, slicker and sea boots. He takes an envelope from inside his hat and slits it with his knife.*)

COLM. "Honestly, I don't remember you, Mr. Primrose. Did we speak to each other at the wedding party? If so, what did we say? I'm sorry I took a month to answer your letter. Please tell the MacAfee "hello" for me. I cannot write any more because I am at work and Mr. Blackstone will be calling for me at any moment. Sincerely, Timothea Stiles." (COLM *reflects.*) *Sincerely*!

(*A week passes. The lights come up on* TIMOTHEA, *again at the mantel, standing as she reads* COLM's *letter and sips from a bowl of soup.*)

COLM. "Did we speak at the wedding party?" Hah! "If so, what did we say?" I was besotted. Oh, Mary. I was leanin' over you, holding myself up with my hands against the wall. You were in a red dress, like *that* in the front. We was discussin' the power of belief.

TIMOTHEA. "And *I* said that the death of a friend

didn't send me skipping off down the street to the All Saints Church. That it made me want to row out more alone in my curragh, maybe, and sit and think. And that could be the same thing, after all."

COLM. You told me as a girl you'd been taught the Catholic faith. So I told you that what I didn't like about that religion was that you had to carry beads with you. And get belittled by another man once a week. A man who went to the toilet same as me. I do not work six days a week to be made small on the seventh. (COLM's *light fades to black.*)

TIMOTHEA. "The great ocean makes be feel small enough."

(*She has been reading with restraint but becomes a bit involved.*)

"Still, don't you find something touching about the sea? It has taken away forever some fine lads and yet I cannot help feeling it could have done more . . ."

(*Cross fade:* TIMOTHEA's *light fades to black;* COLM's *light comes up. A month has passed.* COLM *sits staring over the audience with his chin on his arm. He speaks slowly.*)

COLM. And now He takes away two more men.
God has the power to reason, the sea does not. I cannot understand the teaching in His act and I think I never will. The sea is my religion now and the weather above the sea. Does that sound evil to you, Miss Stiles?

(TIMOTHEA's *light comes up—she is seated in a rocker.*)

COLM. I hope not, because I have not had the chance to sin wondrously. (*He pauses.*) I told the MacAfee "hello" and he says "hello" back to you once again. He told me he never dreamed I would write a letter off to you just like that. I asked him, "Why was that?" He says because he didn't even think I could write a letter.

(COLM's *light fades to black. Another week has passed.*)

TIMOTHEA. "I suppose, then, that my spelling will leave you close to tears as you work for a publisher of books. I hope the sea will be good to us this spring, as good as in summer, which is not far away. If you're not doing anything better, would you write me off another letter, please? Truly yours, Colm Primrose."

(*Cross fade:* TIMOTHEA's *light fades to black.* COLM'S *come up.* COLM *stands, opening a letter, two weeks later.*)

COLM. "I still don't remember you, Mr. Primrose. But that was such a nice letter you wrote me. I feel very sad for your loss. I *don't* think you should call yourself a plain fisherman. Fishermen are important. Just as important as farmers." Hah! "I think you might have a touch of the poet in you, the way Irishmen do. Maybe if you had not become a fisherman you would have been a fine poet." Oh, Mary! "Please say "hello" to the MacAfee for me. I think you write a very nice letter and I *would* like to read another. Truly yours, Timothea Stiles." (COLM *reflects.*)
Truly yours! "I think you write a very *nice letter*!" And you *will* read another. (*He sits and takes a pencil and begins to compose a letter, a word upon a word. He's writing slowly. He writes through her reading of his letter.*)
Dear Miss Stiles, today was not like any other day. The

MacAfee and I were out past the channel and one moment we look up to see that the sky is suddenly black at the west and the clouds are like . . .

(*The lights come up on* TIMOTHEA, *stage right, reading. A week has passed.*)

TIMOTHEA. " . . . great black cats crouched at the edge of the horizon. It looks like a black gale. And while the MacAfee hauls in the lines, I get the head around and put the sail onto her and we start to run home with the gale behind us. I know it'll catch us, but I don't tell the MacAfee . . ."

COLM. (*Writing.*) Who knows the same but doesn't tell me!

TIMOTHEA. "For that is a black gale. We're moving fast—sledding on the waves—but it's moving faster. And just when it's upon us, it goes by, so close we feel the dampness of it. A great cat walking by a mouse it doesn't see! That never happened to us before."

COLM. (*Writing.*) It always catches us and leaves us hanging onto the sides of an upturned curragh.

TIMOTHEA. "An hour later, when we're sailing home, the tank boat comes to see if we need a tow in. But I wave them off. The MacAfee says, Mary-Joseph-and-Christ-in-the-manger, why would you do a thing like that? And I say it's because we can beat them home. And we do! And all the while we're sailing, I'm wondering: Is there going to be a letter from Timothea?"

COLM. And there is a letter! We left that tank boat standing at the Outer Mark! I never had such a day!

TIMOTHEA. "The MacAfee says "hello". I imagine I'll be carrying this conversation between the two of you into next winter. Please write to me if you find the time. Truly yours, Colm." (*She looks up.*) You should take

better care of yourself, Colm.
(*More than a week passes.*)

COLM. I will, I will.
(*Another week passes.*)

TIMOTHEA. The answer is 'yes' to your question. I *would* like you to write to me again. I enjoy hearing about your life at the Heads.
(*A week passes.*)

COLM. I cannot for the life of me know why a city girl like yourself living in a great city such as Liverpool would want to listen to the sludge of a fisherman.

(TIMOTHEA *turns toward him for the first time. Another week has passed. Each speech in their dialogue represents a letter, and each letter represents a week's passage.*)

TIMOTHEA. It's not "sludge" and I'm *not* a city girl.
(*Another week.*)

COLM. It is sludge and you are a city girl.
(*And a week.*)

TIMOTHEA. I'm not!
(*A week.*)

COLM. You said there were a million souls living there with you.
(*A week.*)

TIMOTHEA. But I'm not *from* Liverpool. I'm from Glamorganshire, in Wales . . . (*She jumps to her feet to defend her past with a strong Welsh accent. Another week has passed.*)
We always kept two cows, grew potatoes, green vegs, saw to a bit of hay for winter feeding, cut the fuel, sewed the roof, tended half-dozen hens, provided some butter for the town, baked bread, birthed the piglets. In winter I would light the fire so we could get up in the morning,

crack ice in the basin so we could wash. Ate our porridge with milk still warm from the cow and sausages made only one day out of the pig. But I wouldn't eat the sausages myself, never. The pig would always have been my friend. (*She rests a moment.*) I buried my father. And when I did, I came here. It was a mean little farm in its day, and it provided for my young years. But the roof has fallen in long since. So, you see, I am a bit of a farm girl underneath it all, but I don't let on to everyone I meet.

COLM. Do you think it's that bad?

TIMOTHEA. It wouldn't help my advancement in the publishing business. If I ever get down to London— (*She pauses.*)
Liverpool is a fine place, naturally. There is so much to do here. (TIMOTHEA *is not entirely convinced.*) But I'm counting time so slow this summer. I long for September to come. I don't know why.

(*She tacks* COLM's *letter above the mantel. Her light dims and she holds her position, hand high.* COLM's *light dims. Several months pass.*)

COLM. And September's come and gone. Long since. And it's been a year now we've been writing back and forth.

(*Still holding the letter to the wall, she turns her head to him. A week passes.*)

TIMOTHEA. No! Has it been a year?
(TIMOTHEA's *light fades to black. Another week.*)

COLM. Winter. Spring. Summer. Autumn. Those four make a year, unless I miss my count. (*He opens the window.*) And now winter's nearly passed us once again and this morning I can feel another spring. And I'm still calling you *Miss Stiles.* Not very good progress. Jasus.

(TIMOTHEA'S *light comes up. She is seated on a pillow downstage of the hearth. Time has passed.*)

TIMOTHEA. "And so I was wondering if you'd mind if I wrote to you by your Christian name? Timothea. I hope you don't think that I am in any way trying to court you, after all, two lives could not be more different than ours. But it's such a pretty name, that's all."

(COLM'S *light comes up. Time passes.*)

COLM. Tim-o-thea!

TIMOTHEA. (*Writing.*) "Dearest Colm." No. "*Dear* Colm." I do think it's poetic when you talk about your life at the Heads.

COLM. Hah!

TIMOTHEA. It *is.* "The birds have wingspan but no sense, no feeling." *That's* poetic.

(COLM *thinks, then begins to write. A week passes.*)

COLM. Well, the Heads is a curious place. The sea, against its will, faces the land in a world the sea would have all sea. And the land gives the sea these walls of rock to confound its waves. And so the sea can never sleep.

(TIMOTHEA *continues the letter as a poem. A week has passed.*)

TIMOTHEA. "And the people here are the same.
Oh, they know they are of the land
But also part of the sea,

So they live one leg to the sea
And ride this troubled coast.
Their only sleep is what a man will sleep
Too tired to hear his weariness.
The people here are old;
Even the young, just married, looking out,
Look back upon their cliffs and the ageless
War the sea's declared against their land.
Land's end."
Colm, that's lovely.

COLM. Thank you, Timothea, do you really think so?

TIMOTHEA. Yes, Colm. And you write with words that would never send anyone flying to a dictionary.

COLM. I can't guess why.

TIMOTHEA. I hope you don't mind, but I showed just a little bit of your letter to Mr. Blackstone and he said that's the best kind of writing in the world. (TIMOTHEA *tacks the letter above the mantel. There are others there now. Another week goes by. After a pause, she reads from another letter.*) " . . . if the wind wanted to stay for years, it would. And it has. It blew, I think until I was eleven and then stopped one day and let us be." (TIMOTHEA *tacks it over the mantel.*) I've got to get away from Liverpool! It's so dirty here.

COLM. (*He stops writing and looks up. It is a week later.*) There's always a sea wind blowing here!

TIMOTHEA. (*Another week.*) But it's a long way. I just can't *go* to the Heads.

COLM. Yes you can! (*Uncertainly.*) Can't you?

TIMOTHEA. For one thing, I don't have a holiday.

COLM. Oh.

TIMOTHEA. Besides, how would it look?

COLM. Fine!

TIMOTHEA. (*Suddenly.*) I've never seen you! How would I know what you look like? (*They both pause.*)

COLM. Simple! (*He begins to write.*)

TIMOTHEA. Oh?

COLM. My dear Timothea . . . my *darling* Timothea. I'll make this a short letter . . .

TIMOTHEA. " . . . because I can see through the pane that the moon has settled and the night has almost run out. I wanted to ask you, did you know about a relation of yours who's getting married here?"

COLM. You see there's a wedding planned between Ernest Terrence Feeney, known as 'Red Ernest' and Maggie Swan, who is your *third cousin*. It is to be at the Heads in September. Think of that!

TIMOTHEA. Think of that!

COLM. Well, I wanted to tell you in case you had any thought of coming over for the wedding.

TIMOTHEA. "And now I'd better get to my curragh and out on the water, or the fish will be wondering why I'm so late in coming for them. Can you come to the wedding?"

COLM. I wish you could.

TIMOTHEA. "As ever, Colm." (*Privately.*) I wish I could.

(*Both areas fade to black.*)

ACT ONE

SCENE 2

Night. Onstage are gravestones and a bench. Light comes through a high window and the sound of reels and jigs is heard from the wedding party within. COLM *bursts through an arched doorway with a force that takes him to center stage. He wears a cap, a black jacket, a white shirt buttoned at the neck and his woolen trousers. He goes to a bottle concealed behind a gravestone and takes a swig of potcheen: a home-brewed, colorless whiskey. He does a slight jig as the potcheen reaches his limbs, then braces himself for re-entry to the party.* TIMOTHEA *has entered and stands watching* COLM. *She holds a cup of punch and wears a wool scarf, maybe a hat, and certainly her red dress.* COLM *takes a draught of potcheen, replaces the bottle, shadow boxes, turns upstage with renewed confidence and confronts* TIMOTHEA. *The music, laughter and applause continue during their meeting.*

TIMOTHEA. Colm.

COLM. At last.

(*She tries to maintain gloved party manners.*)

TIMOTHEA. What?

COLM. (*With less confidence.*) At last.

TIMOTHEA. (*Regarding him fully.*) I do remember you now.

COLM. At the punch bowl. Can I fetch you some?

TIMOTHEA. No. Thank you.

COLM. I wouldn't put my arm in it again. (TIMOTHEA *watches.*) Uh, a mug of tea? (TIMOTHEA *says no silently.*) Au, have some punch, then. It's not too strong. It's done nothing for me.

TIMOTHEA. Did you want it to?

COLM. Yes.

TIMOTHEA. Because of meeting me?

COLM. Well, I suppose.

TIMOTHEA. Why?

COLM. Well, that's the thing about me; everytime I meet a lady I've been writing to for a year-and-a-half

I'm apt to take a drop or two.

TIMOTHEA. Did it help you this time?

COLM. Uh. I don't know, really.

TIMOTHEA. Am I different than you remember me?

COLM. Uglier. (*He has made a joke and he laughs.*)

TIMOTHEA. And so are you. (*They both do.*)

COLM. Much. I'd imagined you a certain way and for the longest time I never saw you and so I began wondering if—you know—who—if I was corresponding with who I thought I was corresponding with. And in the letters you always seemed alone—I mean you were not married, and you were not twenty anymore—I began—(*His new confidence flown.*) Can I fetch you a drink of something?

TIMOTHEA. Whiskey. (*She empties the punch glass she has been holding onto the ground.*)

COLM. (*Startled.*) Whiskey?

TIMOTHEA. Thank you.

COLM. (*Delighted.*) I think I know where there's a kirn nearby.

TIMOTHEA. I think you do too.

COLM. I'll fetch us a drop from it. (*He takes a step away and reaches the bottle from behind the stone and pours into her cup until she raises a finger. They drink, looking out. It is an acquired taste, potcheen, antagonistic; at one time more familiar to* TIMOTHEA.)

TIMOTHEA. Winter is coming.

COLM. Ah, it is. It always seems to this time of year. Naturally. (*Pause.*) You confuse me! Do you wonder that I can write you letters but that I cannot speak to you about anything?

TIMOTHEA. You'd be speaking for the both of us. I was very nervous about meeting you.

COLM. Truly? It'll take us some getting used to, I think.

TIMOTHEA. Yes.

(*He leaps to his feet and offers her the bench.*)

COLM. Sit! Some time spent talking.

TIMOTHEA. We might go for a walk.

COLM. Tomorrow, to the Heads! It's a Sunday and it should be fair and calm. We could pack up some food. What do you think? (*She tries to answer.*) No! There's no need. There's an inn on the mainland. The Plow and Anchor. (That's to please both the fishermen and the farm men as well.) I'll row you there and I'll afford you a *good* lunch. It's brisk out and we'd be away from the weather.

TIMOTHEA. I have to leave in the morning.

COLM. I thought you'd stay the week.

TIMOTHEA. Yes, well, this isn't a proper holiday. I just came down for the wedding.

COLM. Oh, I see.

TIMOTHEA. I can't take my week until spring.

COLM. Do they really need you there so much that you can't take a week to refresh your glands, as they say?

TIMOTHEA. They have rules for us.

COLM. I cannot say much for a job that keeps you in one place when you don't want to be.

TIMOTHEA. But I like my job. It's really fascinating. Books come in and sometimes Mr. Blackstone asks me what I think of them.

COLM. Well, that sounds *fascinating* enough. Do they publish histories, by any chance?

TIMOTHEA. Once in a while.

COLM. Ah, I like the stories from history.

TIMOTHEA. Last year we brought out some stories: *Legends from British History for Young Readers.*

COLM. Was there anything from Ireland in those books?

TIMOTHEA. I think there was one on Donegal. And one on—

COLM. Kilkenny?

TIMOTHEA. Yes, I think there was.

COLM. Aaah, I'd like to see *that* book.

TIMOTHEA. When I get back to my job, I'll see if there's one around, and if there is, I'll pack it off to you, express. A present.

COLM. Aaah, that's a fine present. I want to give you something to take back to Liverpool from me.

TIMOTHEA. It's not necessary, Colm.

COLM. Yes, it is, Timothea. (*He gives her a flat, black box he yanks from an inner pocket.*)

TIMOTHEA. Oh. (*She opens it, sees the present and takes a breath.*) It's a pen. (*She sees a small card.*) There's a card. (*She reads it.*) It's a guarantee.

COLM. It's guaranteed!

TIMOTHEA. Thank you.

(*He fills her glass, which is on the bench, and takes a drink himself. He stands looking out. There is a lapse.*)

COLM. We are quite confined here in the winter!

TIMOTHEA. Oh?

COLM. Ah, yes. The winter is longish here. What we do is sew and repair things we use in the summer. We knit.

TIMOTHEA. You knit?

COLM. Well, we knit all manner of things. We knit scarves. We knit hats. If the winter were long enough, we could knit a house. We have readings, and the MacAfee or Mrs. Stoney will read historic stories to us. We sit at a fire and think about what's being read, and we knit. There have been some fine heroes come out of

Ireland. We have a great need to be heroes here.

TIMOTHEA. Oh, I know.

COLM. We go out a dozen times in the winter. There's cod running by outside the channel and it's up to us to catch it. But the oars and gunnels get slick with ice and there's not a way to keep your fingers from turning blue except to grab onto nets and ropes and whatever is at hand. But still it takes you three whiskeys and a long stand in front of the fire at the Captain's before you feel yourself again. I'll tell you how cold it gets you: sometimes you cannot speak. That's how cold it gets you!

TIMOTHEA. Well, Liverpool's not like that. It's so cold sometimes getting to work is a blessing because we can have a cup of tea at the office when we arrive.

COLM. (*Waving the bottle.*) Would you care for a number three?

TIMOTHEA. Thank you, yes. But I work with very pleasant people. It's in a way my other home. I feel as though Mr. Blackstone is my father and I could always ask him for help. Just like the MacAfee is to you, Colm.

COLM. That's a rarity.

TIMOTHEA. Well, he's like your father.

COLM. I never had a true da. (*He sees something off and away, just above the audience but below the horizon; through the back wall of the theater.*)

TIMOTHEA. I know that, Colm.

COLM. So, it's really not so much of a grind as you make out.

TIMOTHEA. That's right. I should be more thankful than I am. But there's more to living than a good job.

COLM. But don't you see that you're stuck there for as long as they say?

TIMOTHEA. A woman doesn't mind that so much as a man.

COLM. I don't think so. She couldn't. If I felt that about my life here, well, it would be a slow death for me. (COLM *has been watching something on the water.*) Now who do you suppose is out there?

TIMOTHEA. What?

COLM. There's a boat out there on the water.

TIMOTHEA. Where?

COLM. Out there! Can you not see the boat?

TIMOTHEA. No.

COLM. Stand up here.

(TIMOTHEA *crosses to* COLM. *They stare off together, as though they were on a rise above the sea.*)

COLM. It's Smiggy and Pete! What's those fools doing out there tonight. Doesn't they know there's a wedding party going on?

TIMOTHEA. I can't see any boat.

(COLM *looks at her until she turns to him.*)

COLM. No?

TIMOTHEA. No.

COLM. I don't think you've got the eyes for it. You've got city eyes.

(*She stands looking up at him.*)

TIMOTHEA. Have you ever left the Heads?

COLM. I go to Galway each winter to meet the fisheries trawler and each winter we sail up to the ice, seeing sights not many people have seen. Have you ever seen an emerald glacier standing up from the water?

TIMOTHEA. No.

COLM. Well, we see them all the time up at the Circle.

(TIMOTHEA *moves away from him.*)

TIMOTHEA. Have you ever been to Liverpool?

COLM. What for? I want to have a reason to go somewhere; not just go to see a place I don't know.

TIMOTHEA. As long as you don't need to see other places, that must mean you're very happy here.

COLM. Well, I'm content. I'm a content person. I think. Do you find it helps you to be happy to travel? Where have you gotten to?

TIMOTHEA. I've been to Scotland and France; Paris. And London. I just can't believe that you have never left this place, really.

COLM. Well, I can leave any time I want. I mean even when the fish are running, I can say—let 'em run. I'm going for a walk in the mountains.

TIMOTHEA. Have you ever said that?

COLM. No. I never have said that.

TIMOTHEA. You never said to someone, "Use my boat. I'm going away for awhile. I'll be back when I'll be back?"

COLM. That would be a hardship on the MacAfee.

TIMOTHEA. But you've never said that?

COLM. No, I haven't, for the love of God!

TIMOTHEA. Well, you see? It's just like you had a job and bosses the same as me.

COLM. I'm free to go when I choose. I just have never chosen, that's all.

TIMOTHEA. Would you like to?

COLM. Leave?

TIMOTHEA. Yes.

COLM. But to go where?

TIMOTHEA. Liverpool.

COLM. When?

TIMOTHEA. Whenever you can.
COLM. Do you want me to come to Liverpool, then?
TIMOTHEA. Yes, Colm.
COLM. Would I be visiting you?
TIMOTHEA. Yes, Colm.
COLM. And where would I stay in Liverpool?
TIMOTHEA. With me.

(*The lights fade to black. Sounds of travel over land and water blend into the traffic sounds of Liverpool.*)

ACT ONE

SCENE 3

Night. TIMOTHEA'S *flat in Liverpool; a curiosity. It is on the third storey of a stone Victorian mansion that has been split up into flats. In the 19th century, hers was part of a formal music room and its gaudy mouldings now collide with the wall of an added kitchen. There is a raised area upstage, a platform, where* TIMOTHEA *sleeps, and behind it is a bay window through which the weather and the time of day can be seen. At certain times, traffic noise comes from there, too.* TIMOTHEA *has decorated it as a woman of some illusions might, but her bright illusions are timid against the pretentious structure and conflict with its dark, high-ceilinged style. A round table has been moved to the center of the room and has been set for dinner. The meal is finished and a lone candle gutters in its stand. There is a light seen in the kitchen and a lamp lit by the bed upstage.* COLM'S *sea bag and tin chest are on the floor, downstage. He sits back from the table facing the candle holding a napkin.* TIMOTHEA *is up, clearing away the dishes.*

COLM. So that's a ragout of beef, is it?

TIMOTHEA. Have you never heard of it?

COLM. Well, yes, I've heard of it. Just never had it was all. Now I've had it. (*He gets a pipe from his sea bag.*) Very good.

TIMOTHEA. I'm glad you liked my first meal.

COLM. Then I'll have to make you my stew one night. But it must only be cooked in a dirty pot, one that's had years of fish cooking in it.

TIMOTHEA. Can I get you any more of anything?

(COLM *goes to his jacket on the coat tree for his pouch.*)

COLM. No, no, no. I'm having my pipe now.

TIMOTHEA. Colm.

COLM. What?

TIMOTHEA. Nothing. Not a thing. I'm just saying your name: Colm. (TIMOTHEA *folds one side of the table and moves it against the wall.*)

COLM. Timothea.

That'll take some getting used to, I think.

TIMOTHEA. There never was a nickname for Timothea. You either said it, or you didn't.

COLM. I'll say it then. Timothea.

TIMOTHEA. Would you like a cup of tea, Colm?

COLM. No! Thank you.

TIMOTHEA. I'll get some stout tomorrow.

COLM. It's good with Guinness!

Long trip.

(*She has lit incense from the candle and walks the stick around the room, conducting.*)

TIMOTHEA. Wasn't it? Bus, train, boat and bus again. Wasn't the Isle of Man pretty?

COLM. Pretty? Well, yes it was. Part pretty, part something more. (*He watches her warily.*) What's that smell?

TIMOTHEA. That's incense.

COLM. Oh.

TIMOTHEA. Don't look so put off, Colm—it's to make the room smell pretty.

COLM. But I don't think it does.

TIMOTHEA. Then I'll put it out. (*She crosses toward the kitchen. He jumps up.*)

COLM. No, no, no. Job! I didn't mean that. I meant it didn't suit me, yet. There's a lot, you know, that'll take me getting used to.

TIMOTHEA. I know, Colm. I can see that. (TIMOTHEA *takes a step toward him.*) Would you excuse me please?

COLM. Naturally I would.

(*She exits upstage into the bathroom.*)

I mean I like cooking smells! (*Aside:*) It smells like a Catholic Church in here. (*He lights his pipe from the candle and then calls to her from the hearth.*) We have a little saying at the Heads: "If you use your own tobacco it's wasteful. If you use your neighbor's, you stuff your pipe so full it will not draw!" (*He has made a joke, chuckles, waits for a reaction, hears none, stares at the bed.*) Just the one bed?

TIMOTHEA. (*Voice.*) Yes, Colm.

COLM. Cozy spot.

(*She enters in a robe and crosses to the heater and turns it off.*)

TIMOTHEA. My landlady says this used to be a music room about a hundred years ago. (*She turns the bed lamp off, winds the alarm clock, turns down her side of the bed and then, after looking at him, his side.*) I'm sleepy, Colm.

COLM. (COLM, *sitting at the table, stares out.*) But, I'll tell you one thing that'll set you back a bit, miss. You are talking to—what you have before you—is a thirty-five-year-old *spinster-man.

TIMOTHEA. What?

COLM. That's what I am saying to you; I'm a spinster. An old maid. Never been deflowered, as they say.

TIMOTHEA. But, you mean never?

COLM. Never.

TIMOTHEA. Don't make the chickens laugh! (COLM *is wounded.*) Not ever once?

COLM. Not ever once. Promise.

TIMOTHEA. Oh, Colm. You don't have to say that to me. Thank you for your concern, but you musn't say things you think I want to hear. Women are different; they like a man to be experienced. Somewhat.

COLM. Then you'll have to look for another man, won't you? Because I am not experienced. Somewhat.

TIMOTHEA. Truly?

COLM. Yes, yes! For the love of God! I'm a virgin man and there'll be no use me pretending any different because soon enough you'll know. So why deceive you into thinking I'm some kind of man of the world, as they say.

TIMOTHEA. You're the one who's being deceived, Colm Primrose. That's the kind of man I don't want. Anymore. (*She takes her robe off and lays it on the bed and stands by her side of the bed in a feminine, white nightgown.*)

*(*Subject to casting, of course.*)

COLM. What do you call that you're wearing?
TIMOTHEA. A nightdress.
COLM. I suppose there's nothing more to say.
TIMOTHEA. No, Colm.

(*He edges a step toward her.*)

COLM. So. And without further fussing around, I will take you abed.
TIMOTHEA. Yes, Colm.

(*He moves another step or two, pulls off his vest and hangs it on the coat tree.*)

COLM. And of course you realize I've had no previous schooling, here, in the task we're about to perform.
TIMOTHEA. Yes, Colm.

(*He takes another step.*)

COLM. And that I'm taking my chances here, same as you.
TIMOTHEA. Yes, Colm.

(*Almost to the bed,* COLM *suddenly wheels back to the hearth.*)

COLM. Hey! I wonder what Smiggy and Pete are doing *right now*? They're probably coming in right about now, all wet, and smelling like cods. Ha! Smiggy and Pete, what clowns! What would they do if they could catch a glimpse of us right now? (*He sits down in the rocker, speaking too quickly.*) You know, after Twelfth Night, some of us go for cod until March? We get up to the Arctic Circle. The fisheries trawler picks us up down to Galway. You must sign on by letter in advance. We always go. We're the only ones from the Heads that *do* go. Of course, the MacAfee doesn't any more because of his age. One gets to see many things on these trips that one is deprived of if he were to stay landbound for the entire winter. For example: sleeping whales. Now that's a thing to see! They've mostly been killed and so it's long between sightings, but when you see one there, great beast, sleeping just at the surface, your heart grows soft and you think – who is it that kills that great beast? And what for?

(TIMOTHEA *has gradually crossed to* COLM *and she now kneels beside his chair and he slows and stops, still holding his heart. She stretches from her knees to kiss him just behind the cheek.*)

COLM. I imagine I should remove my trousers.

TIMOTHEA. Yes, Colm.

COLM. I think that would better be done in the dark.

TIMOTHEA. Yes, Colm. (*She goes to the table and blows out the candle. The stage goes dark.*)

ACT ONE

SCENE 4

The same night, two hours later. Street sounds are heard and the street light of Liverpool comes up through the window. COLM *is seated in the window seat, outlined by the city loom.* TIMOTHEA *wakes up.*

TIMOTHEA. Colm?

COLM. Yes?

TIMOTHEA. Where are you? (*She turns the light on and sits up. He is in his socks and underwear and looks miserable. He has her robe pulled around him. It is cold.*) Are you awake?

COLM. Yes.

TIMOTHEA. *Were* you awake?

COLM. Before, you mean?

TIMOTHEA. Yes.

COLM. I'm sorry.

TIMOTHEA. For what?

COLM. For falling off to sleep.

TIMOTHEA. You were so tired.

COLM. What time is it? It must be almost morning.

TIMOTHEA. (*Picks up clock.*) Eleven thirty.

COLM. (*Indicates street.*) Do they leave the lights on all night?

TIMOTHEA. No. Yes.

COLM. Did I hurt you? (*She doesn't answer.*) Before. I did. Didn't I?

TIMOTHEA. No, Colm, not really.

COLM. I think I was eager.

TIMOTHEA. I think I was nervous.

COLM. It wasn't right, was it?

TIMOTHEA. It was the first time.

COLM. For me.

TIMOTHEA. For us. Too. Maybe that was it.

(COLM *crosses from the window seat to the hearth.*)

COLM. But it wasn't even a first *time* for us. Was it?

TIMOTHEA. Almost. I think you scared me.

COLM. It was all over so quick! (*He pauses.*) I hurt myself.

TIMOTHEA. Where?

COLM. I'm sure I'm going to recover.
Aren't I?

TIMOTHEA. Yes.

COLM. You know, it's damned sorry—pitiful—that you're after teaching me what I ought, by rights, to be teaching you. I'm not talking about fishing.

TIMOTHEA. I don't think I'll have to teach you any more.

COLM. Should I come back?

TIMOTHEA. Yes.

COLM. But there's no room. We are packed in there like herring.

TIMOTHEA. It's alright.

COLM. What woke you? (*Starts to stand and sits.*) Would you turn that off, please?

(*She does, and the stage returns to night.*)

ACT ONE

SCENE 5

Slowly, morning lightens the bay window, turning the far wall to yellow. TIMOTHEA *is seated in the bay window studying* COLM, *who is on the bed, in deep sleep, turned away from the audience. A chill is felt in the room;* TIMOTHEA *has not yet lit the heater. Street sounds begin to swell. She calls to him, gently.*

TIMOTHEA. Colm? Colm? (*She crosses to the foot of the bed and tugs his leg, making sure that he's asleep;*

when she's certain he is, she talks to him.) And *you* are the first boy who had *me*. It was you, Colm. You're the boy. (TIMOTHEA *becomes Welsh, once again, speaking in an accent.*) He was always trying something with me in the barn, grabbing at me and so forth. Always trying to show me what he had for me. Waiting for me places. You're that same boy. All of him you.

The boy and me had been delivering a calf, see?, and it was not a good birthing, you see? It was a bloody, bloody mess. It wasn't raining, but there was mist coming in through the cracks in the great door of the barn. The boy and me had been working at it a long time. The boy said she was to die but the good cow would *not* die. And when the calf came, it was weak, but fine. Oh, Jesus, fine, fine, fine.

(*Perhaps she takes his jacket and holds it around her.*)

It stood up and the boy cut it off from its ma, see? She tried to turn around to look at her calf for the first time but she couldn't get up, so much had been taken out of her. She tried to lick her calf but she couldn't get her legs under her. So the calf toddles over to its mother's face so it could be licked.

(TIMOTHEA *gets up, looks again at* COLM, *and goes to the hearth and lights it; warms herself, front and back.*)

There was blood all around. We didn't know which was to live or die. There's nothing to do with a cow—you must let cows decide how much they want to live. We were so tired.

(*She pauses.*)

I let the boy have me then. It was up in the hay loft—you might have expected that—and he seized me. (*Pause.*) You're the boy. That boy was you. And all the time we was doing it up there, there was blood on us from the cow. Blood on his arms he was pinning me down with. Then there was my blood. Too.

I just wanted to tell you that.

(COLM *has awakened and is quietly watching her.*) And do you know what? *That* boy couldn't even write his name.

(COLM *lets the moment stand, realizing some of what she has said, maybe understanding the idea of it. He props his head up and smiles at her.*)

COLM. How'd the cow make out?

TIMOTHEA. Oh, she lived. (*She hestitates, then goes to the bed and starts to undress.*)

ACT ONE

SCENE 6

Early evening; winter light. COLM *is alone onstage; he sits on his tin chest, sewing his sea bag. He hasn't turned a light on yet but curses the dimness. Empty bottles of stout stand on the round table, center stqge.* TIMOTHEA *enters after a few moments, with her string bag full of crab, baked rolls, potatoes and stout.*

TIMOTHEA. I'm here, Colm. (*She turns on a light and stands center stage. They grin at each other.*)

COLM. Hello.

TIMOTHEA. Hello. (*She goes to him but they do not kiss or touch.*) What are you doing?

COLM. I'm sewing my bag.

TIMOTHEA. But I can do that.

COLM. No, no. I always sew my bag myself.

TIMOTHEA. I see you went out today. (*She pulls out a*

bottle.) I brought you the same. (*She crosses to the kitchen.*) I brought you a surprise, Colm.

COLM. Thank you Timothea.

TIMOTHEA. Don't you want to know what it is?

COLM. Yes, please.

TIMOTHEA. Well, I won't give it to you now. After supper.

COLM. It's a gift?

TIMOTHEA. I don't know.

COLM. How can you not know?

TIMOTHEA. Only you can tell me whether it's a gift or not.

COLM. What *is* it?

TIMOTHEA. I'll give it to you after supper. Where did you go today?

COLM. I only got as far as the corner and a pair of yobs begged a shilling out of me. Then I went to a pub and another one wanted to have a fight.

TIMOTHEA. You had a fight?

(COLM *does a brisk pantomine of a fight as he crosses to the kitchen.*)

COLM. I didn't see the reason of it.

TIMOTHEA. Good, I'm glad.

COLM. I mean, you don't fight with strangers, do you. Did you get to your job alright?

TIMOTHEA. I got there during lunch. Everyone was gone. I felt like a schoolgirl who'd been bad. (*She lights the heater and sits by it.*)

COLM. I'm sorry.

TIMOTHEA. No, Colm! I loved it.

COLM. Did you tell them why you were late?

TIMOTHEA. No! I just said that I was tired from my

trip. They knew I'd been off somewhere for the weekend. I think a couple of the girls would like my job.

(COLM *stares at her across the stage until she turns to him.*)

COLM. Timothea, would you like to tell me why you haven't said that your husband is working at the publisher's with you?

TIMOTHEA. He's not my husband. He's my ex.

COLM. Well, would you carry on please and tell me the rest of what I want to know?

TIMOTHEA. He works in the same building as me. Yes, that's true. But he doesn't work in the office.

COLM. The last I heard he was in jail for wrong-doing or some such.

TIMOTHEA. Yes. Well, he's been at Blackstone's only a few months.
I mean I don't run into him every day.

COLM. Well, I do. He came by at midday.

TIMOTHEA. Here?

COLM. Yes. He dropped 'round—he called on me sort of—told me you weren't at work yet and that he was "concerned."
Well, I don't mind saying it, he seemed a right nice fellow.

TIMOTHEA. You got *on* with him?

COLM. Well, yes I did.

TIMOTHEA. He can be very nice, sometimes.

COLM. Then why didn't you get on? Because I fancy that you're very nearly the perfect lady—the fisherman's dream.

TIMOTHEA. He had bad tendencies. He liked to finagle people out of the things they owned.

COLM. Well, I know. He told me about Manchester

where he was all these past two years. We divided six pints of Guinness. I told him that if he would ever consider fishing as a trade, I told him that I would be pleased to guide him.

TIMOTHEA. You told him that? What did he say?

COLM. He said alright, fine, he would.

TIMOTHEA. You were too good to him. I mean he was a confidence man. He could talk you as far as that! (*She indicates a distance.*)

COLM. Well, yes, but what's he doing now?

TIMOTHEA. He's in the binding plant.

COLM. I think fishing's better than that, even for a confidence man.

TIMOTHEA. I think you're probably right.

COLM. He sailed right in here with a "Hello, there, mate, how's yourself?" Familiar.

TIMOTHEA. He knows how to cover his surprise.

COLM. Well, you'd better tell him a word or two tomorrow, Timothea. So that he won't be "coming over to tea" all the time.

TIMOTHEA. I will, I definitely will.

COLM. I'm not vexed. But he doesn't belong here. That's right, now.

TIMOTHEA. I will tell him.

COLM. He seems to be a man of affairs without question.
Where's my gift?

TIMOTHEA. *After* supper.

COLM. Well, let's eat this supper. What'd you get?

TIMOTHEA. I picked up two crab and we'll have potatoes and ale along with them. (*She brings a crab from the kitchen and waves it at him. He grabs it and smells it, nods, and returns it.*)

COLM. Regular Irish, aren't we?

TIMOTHEA. Well, I wanted to make you a dish you knew, after all.

COLM. It'll seem strange eating this here. We always had it at the Captain's on a Sunday afternoon.

TIMOTHEA. You'll just have to pretend that this is Sunday at the Heads.

COLM. That it is not.

TIMOTHEA. I haven't bothered with cooking much for awhile.

COLM. Then I'll have to give you a try of my fish stew. It's a simple dish made of anything that swims stuffed into an iron pot and cooked on a turf hearth. I'd make the lot and in the winter it might last a week. But in the summer, after a couple of days it would get a little fur covering on it, sort of like a muff. And that's the part you wouldn't eat.

(*She sets the table and brings in a candle. The room has dimmed; she lights it.*)

TIMOTHEA. It'll be fine cooking for you. I hate cooking for myself. I usually stand up when I eat alone. (*She is about to place the candle, when she stops and stares into the flame.*) And sometimes I'd get scared that I might spend the rest of my life standing up, eating alone. And there'd be no one here who could really take me out of myself. I'd get cold standing at the mantel, and have crazy feelings that someone was watching me. So I'd just *be* here, scared, and not do anything about it and pretty soon it'd pass and I'd go to bed, but my sleep would be strange. I'd wake up in the morning and feel lost again. I think I'm lonelier in the morning than I am the night before.
I think the morning is the smartest time not to be alone.

COLM. (*Newly informed.*) The smartest time not to be alone is when you're dropping off to sleep.

TIMOTHEA. I can remember that feeling right now, but not the scare of it.

COLM. Where's my gift?

TIMOTHEA. (*She stands in the kitchen doorway.*) I wanted the moment to be one that you'll always remember. Because you might not ever speak to me again.

COLM. What is it?

TIMOTHEA. (*From her purse she brings out a small, flat package.*) Here it is, Colm.

COLM. Small for the excitement. (*He unwraps it.*) "*Sea Sonnets*?" (*He turns some pages, smells them.*) Why, what a pretty thing it is! (*He goes to her and gives her a kiss.*) And I thank you. (*He puts the book down.*) Can I get myself another ale? (*He enters the kitchen.* TIMOTHEA *turns upstage.*)

TIMOTHEA. Read one to me, please.

COLM. Now?

TIMOTHEA. Yes, Colm. Please.

COLM. Which? There are so many here.

TIMOTHEA. Any one.

COLM. "The people here are old. Even the young, just married, looking out, look back upon—their—cliffs—" (*"Their cliffs" takes him longer to say than the other words. He closes the book; sees his name on the cover.*) What. Is. This.

TIMOTHEA. Are you happy?

COLM. (*Stunned.*) *Sea Sonnets*, by Colm Primrose.

TIMOTHEA. You look as if you're going to be sick, Colm.

COLM. (*Slowly, finding his way among the pages, fascinated.*) I truly don't know how I feel, but I know I never felt like this. "This is my country, the sea country." That was from a letter I wrote you. (*He turns to another page.*) "When the storm had blown itself away, the cows came down from the hills—lean and wildeyed—they surely stepped along the road—and found their owners' meadows strewn, familiar." So was *that*!

TIMOTHEA. Everything in the book is from your letters, Colm. From the entire winter and summer.

(COLM *is bewildered and becoming upset.*)

COLM. What? The letters I wrote you are in this book?

TIMOTHEA. There's nothing personal in the book, Colm. I mean nothing personal that you wrote me.

COLM. Is that why you were writing to me?

TIMOTHEA. You're a grand writer, Colm.

COLM. I learned to hold a pencil for you!

TIMOTHEA. Mr. Blackstone says there's not many can coax meanings out of words the way you can.
It's a grand gift.

COLM. It's not a gift. I only tried my best to please you. But it seems strange to me looking at them now, in the stone, like a grave, lasting.

TIMOTHEA. It's something permanent, Colm.

COLM. "Sea Sonnets"—and what the hell is a sonnet?

TIMOTHEA. A poem.

COLM. I don't write poems and here I am a poet. Is there a pint anywhere close at hand? (*He drops or throws the book and crosses to the kitchen with his empty glass.*)

TIMOTHEA. I bought some wine.

COLM. Poets don't drink ale?

TIMOTHEA. Wine is for celebrations. (TIMOTHEA *waits a moment.*) Is it a celebration?

(COLM *takes the book up again and considers it.*

There is more to this than he is willing to consider at the moment. But he shrugs it off.)

COLM. God, yes! Let's celebrate this book. I am a poet – The Poet of Cliffhorn Heads.

TIMOTHEA. The poet of Cliffhorn Heads.

COLM. I never heard of such a thing! One foot to the sea, the other in Liverpool. Timothea Stiles you knock the pegs out from under me and I love you for that! (*He grabs her and crushes her, then goes and picks up the book again and studies it.*) I would have called it "Sea Voices." (*He pauses.*) I would have called it "Sea Marks." Yes, "Sea Marks!" Those lines that the highest reach of the tide leave on the land to remind you that it'll be back.

TIMOTHEA. I think I like that much better.

COLM. Well, naturally you do.
Half-a-pound! You mean they're selling the thing? What if nobody buys one?

TIMOTHEA. Oh, Colm.

(*He sits on the bed, studying the book.* TIMOTHEA *gets the wine from the kitchen and takes it to the center table and opens it.* COLM *abruptly quietens.*)

COLM. They call me a "primitive" here. (*He indicates book flap.*)

TIMOTHEA. I know.

(*A shock of recognition flashes through him. But he only lets it stay a moment.*)

COLM. (*Quietly.*) Is that what I am to them, then, a primitive? (*He pauses, lowers his voice.*) Blast, I am, you know. I am a primitive. (*Recovers.*) And what the hell are they who have never dragged nets for their dinners, who run like schools every day to jobs I never knew were needed. I think that they go through the same—what's the word I need?

TIMOTHEA. Rituals.

COLM. —that *we* do. Only it seems to me they dress up for theirs. (*She sits beside him and gives him a glass.*) I can't say I like the pictures. Whoever made these pictures has never been to the Heads. That's a certainty.

TIMOTHEA. Probably not, Colm, not many people have been there.

COLM. But it's all described in the book. I don't think the lady drew these has ever seen the sea.

TIMOTHEA. It's a man.

COLM. Fancy that!
Darlin' pictures! Well, no one but me will ever know if they're right or wrong. I don't think I'd want any of my chums leafin' through these pages.

TIMOTHEA. You ought to be proud. This book might make you famous.

COLM. They'd run me out. I'm calling them what they are and they won't like that. People don't.

TIMOTHEA. But you're calling yourself what you are, too. You're putting yourself in among them.

COLM. Where I belong.

TIMOTHEA. Where you once belonged.

COLM. No, where I belong.

TIMOTHEA. Now you belong here, with me.
(*She pauses.*) Don't you?
(*She waits.*) Don't you?

COLM. (*After a long pause.*) That's right, love. I belong here, with you. (*He pauses.*)
My stomach's barkin' for food—where in hell is that supper?

(*Lights dim to black.*)

END OF ACT ONE

ACT TWO

SCENE 1

Late afternoon a month later. COLM *sits alone onstage. Beside him on the table is a stack of "Sea Sonnets." He signs copies intermittently and tosses them into a carton at his feet. Dance music has been playing from a small radio on the mantel and he finally responds to it by snapping it off. He crosses up to the window, which is open, then drifts back downstage. He speaks to the MacAfee, composing* a letter.

COLM. Well, MacAfee, here I am.
Gone longer than the two weeks, am't I?
There's buckets of water between me and you, my dear father; and you alone, doing the work for the both of us. You're strong enough. And there's a good bottom between you and the water, remember, she's sound, that black bitch.
You've a good man in Liam to shove you off the beach. Or if Liam's gone out, there's always Redmond. Just lookyou for that second wave—the one with a broken top would always catch us!
So.
She's a good woman, Timothea, but now I wonder what I'm to do in this city of hers. It's her city, and the city's a woman's place to be, after all. I mean you can't be a man in the city; you can't use yourself well as a man.
I've been wanting to ask her what she'd like to do about our future life together. I think she's a woman to cut the toes off a man. And I don't know what's for it. Still,

don't you need a woman in the house? If it's only to wet your tea, don't you need her there?

(TIMOTHEA *enters, spilling objects: a long mailing tube, a wrapped ream of paper, an umbrella half-closed, her string bag full of lettuce, bottles, fruit, a fish. Her entrance is made with energy and flourish.*)

TIMOTHEA. Colm! Close the window! You're mad as a brush!

(COLM *obeys.* TIMOTHEA *lights the gas heater. She stands and unrolls a poster from the tube and hangs it on the mantel, held by the radio. It is a black-and-white picture of a rocky coastline with a man, seated among the rocks, apparently looking out to sea. "Sea Sonnets" is emblazoned along its top. Along the bottom; "By Colm Primrose" and "Blackstone's Ltd. December 1."* TIMOTHEA *unveils it with style.*)

TIMOTHEA. This is you!

(COLM *regards it briefly.*)

COLM. It's not.
TIMOTHEA. It is.
COLM. It's someone else.
TIMOTHEA. Oh, the *man* isn't you. He *represents* you.
COLM. Right.
TIMOTHEA. The whole idea is you. The image. Isn't it a grand picture?
COLM. (*Without feeling.*) Grand.

TIMOTHEA. Do you have any idea where we're having dinner tonight?
Mr. Blackstone wants us to come to his house. He's sending his car! Oh, Colm, I've never been to his house!

COLM. Oh.

TIMOTHEA. Please hurry up and let's get ready, Colm. Wear your new trousers.

COLM. (*Picks up the ream.*) And what's all this?

TIMOTHEA. That? Writing paper.

COLM. For me?

TIMOTHEA. For you.

COLM. From Mr. Blackstone.

TIMOTHEA. Yes, my darling.

COLM. There must be hundreds of leaves here.

TIMOTHEA. Five hundred exactly.

COLM. (*Returning to the poster.*) That doesn't look like me at all.

(TIMOTHEA *sets* COLM'S *pants on the bed.*)

TIMOTHEA. Please get ready. (TIMOTHEA *is dressing throughout the scene into her familiar red dress.*)

COLM. He's sitting on kelp.
That's not something I'm apt to do. No one with a berry of sense is going to sit on a stack of seaweed.

(*She stops her activity.*)

TIMOTHEA. He's sort of squatting, isn't he?

COLM. What's he supposed to be doing?

TIMOTHEA. He's thinking. Dreaming.

COLM. Squatting.
It's a picture of a fool. (*Drops ream of paper.*) Please tell Mr. Blackstone I could never write so many letters.

To anyone, not even you.

TIMOTHEA. How do you know for sure?

COLM. I know that's all.

TIMOTHEA. There's other things to write beside letters.

COLM. Such as what?

TIMOTHEA. He was hoping you'd see some things here that touched you.

COLM. There's a bunch of yobs out there cockstrutting around the streets and one of these mornings I'm going to have myself a barney. Am I to write about that?

TIMOTHEA. What about all the grand things you've done at the Heads?

COLM. I fished herring and mackerel with a net.
I'm here now.

TIMOTHEA. You could invent stories.

COLM. I'm not the kind that can invent stories and such like that.

(TIMOTHEA *indicates or maybe touches the poster hanging from the mantel.*)

TIMOTHEA. But this is *you*.

COLM. It *represents* me.

TIMOTHEA. Would you like to look for work?

COLM. I notice they don't hand Irish people their jobs here. They're careful about that.
And what would I do then? You don't see 'em making sets along the Mersey River, do you?

TIMOTHEA. You don't ever want to write anymore?

COLM. I don't know.

TIMOTHEA. Don't you aspire to do anything with the rest of your life beside fish for herring and mackerel with a net?

COLM. Well, I do and I don't.
If you mean sit at a table all day long and *aspire*, then I don't.

TIMOTHEA. Don't you want to move people with your words?

COLM. Move what people? Do I know these people?

TIMOTHEA. No. They're the people you were just talking about who sit at tables every day of their lives.

COLM. I can't know what it would be like writing to those poor sots. I have no crow to pluck with them.

TIMOTHEA. Didn't you like writing letters to me?

COLM. Yes, darlin', I did.

TIMOTHEA. Well, write to me and I'll let them pass through me into their hearts.

COLM. God, will you listen to the mouth on the woman. What a lovely way of sayin' it.
You're not talking about the heart, you're talking about the soul. That's the true man *inside* the man, the man who always speaks the truth.
I've seen him die before the man once or twice, leaving the man stranded.
That's an awful sight to see.

TIMOTHEA. Colm, part of love is needing things you never knew you needed. Changing and growing.

COLM. Can't you just go over to Mr. Blackstone's and leave me here?

TIMOTHEA. I told him you'd come.

COLM. *Did* you?

TIMOTHEA. The promotion man will be there, too. He wants to meet you and find out your personality.
He has an idea he'll tell you. Oh, it's a grand idea.

COLM. *Is* it, now?

TIMOTHEA. If I tell you, would you come? (COLM *doesn't answer.*)

TIMOTHEA. I shouldn't tell you. He wanted to. So you must act surprised when he does.
He thinks you ought to read from your book to the Wednesday Afternoon Club. Next week!

COLM. I would never do that!

TIMOTHEA. (*Reverts to Welsh.*) Colm, for the love of God! You drink your pint, you eat your meal, you sit around here sucking on that pipe of yours like a goutish old man.

COLM. Gouty, I think.

TIMOTHEA. Right. Like a gouty old man.

COLM. I do, do I? Well, I'm your gouty old man. After all, you found me, didn't you?

TIMOTHEA. I did, did I? It was me started writing letters to you, I suppose?

COLM. It was you started bringing 'em out in books.

TIMOTHEA. Wsht!

(*They do not speak for a long time; but not more than half a minute.*)

COLM. I think you can say goutish. I've heard goutish.

TIMOTHEA. Anyway, it's an affliction of the joints.

COLM. Not among men who've done real work. Only for those who sit around at table all day long is it an affliction of the joints.

TIMOTHEA. This is a chance to be respected and maybe be paid for it.

COLM. I don't know, Timothea.

TIMOTHEA. Are you a masochist?

COLM. Pardon?

TIMOTHEA. A mas-o-chist. Someone who likes to suffer?

COLM. Right! I would think I am. That's what's become of me, alright.
What did you expect me to become? What you fancied in me was what you read in my soul. Well, it's my soul needs to breathe a little. It's been too long off the water and there's nothing for me to do but remember it. (*He turns.*) I do love you very much my darlin' and I sup-

pose I'm dyin' a bit because of that love—a slow way of dyin'. (*He takes a moment.*) What'll I wear?

TIMOTHEA. Your new trousers! I've had your jersey cleaned. (*She brings him an opaque plastic bag with his sweater in it.*) And *not* those socks.

COLM. Them are good socks.

TIMOTHEA. Yes they are. (*She lifts his foot and pulls one off and runs her arm through the toe hole.*) You can put them on at either end. (*She crosses to the bathroom.*) I'll be out in 10 minutes, Colm. If the driver comes, offer him a glass. And when we're at the house, for the love of God, don't throw your lit matches into the wastepaperbaskets.

(COLM *carefully opens the plastic bag and sees his sweater is now gleaming white.*)

COLM. (*To himself.*) I didn't know it was white. (COLM *tugs the sweater on and stands in front of the mirror over the mantel or at the coat rack. Not only is it dead white, but it has been shrunk to a new size. He poses, adjusting himself to the sweater, rather than the sweater to him, and regards his reflection with a look that might easily be confused with injured vanity.*)

END OF SCENE 1

ACT TWO

SCENE 2

The stage is dark. From the stairs and hallway comes a dreadful harmony and then the sound of TIMOTHEA *trying to shush* COLM. *When they enter the flat and snap on the light,* TIMOTHEA *is seen to be wearing the red dress from the previous scene as well as* COLM's *too-large cap. Her accent is pure Welsh. The tune is "The Foggy Dew" (Irish) and sung briskly.*

COLM AND TIMOTHEA. (*Offstage.*)
The night that Paddy Murphy died
I never will forget
We all got stinking drunk that night
There's some ain't sober yet
The only thing we did that night

(*They enter.* TIMOTHEA *alternately shushing and laughing. Both are drunk.*)

COLM. To fill our hearts with cheer
Was take some ice off Paddy's corpse

TIMOTHEA AND COLM. And put it in our beer.

(COLM *strides to the window, throws it open and yells down to the street.*)

COLM. Safe home, James boyo! (*He slams the window shut.*) Imagine! He brought us all the way home. What a fine steersman that fellow was. That chauffeur.

TIMOTHEA. James.

COLM. Irish. (*He starts back to the window.*)

TIMOTHEA. No, Colm.

COLM. Right! Takin' us through the reef to safe home. We sailed home alright with a bagful of wind in our sails.
How did I behave, hmph? You didn't catch me throwing a single lit match in a wastepaperbasket.

TIMOTHEA. You spat in them instead.
Shame for you, and you under his roof! But I think they liked you anyway.

COLM. Old Blackstone. He's a good man entirely. I'll have a quick glass to your friendship, sir. (*He crosses to the kitchen.*) That promotion man – I'm not sure about him.

TIMOTHEA. He was only doing his job, you know.

COLM. He had a gob on him! What was that he called me? What in hell was it came out of the man?

(TIMOTHEA *laughs, remembering.*)

TIMOTHEA. He called you a horizon-eyed fisherman.

COLM. Perfect! (*This seems unreasonably funny to both of them. He shares his glass.*)

TIMOTHEA. I could see the change in you when he called you that.

COLM. Jasus, what pretty words! Its words like that makes riddles out of feelings. If that's poetry, it's not exactly what I'm after.

TIMOTHEA. You are my horizon-eyed fisherman.

COLM. No more, no less.

TIMOTHEA. Come, be my horizon-eyed fisherman for tonight. (*She goes to him and holds him. He separates himself to replenish his glass.*)

COLM. I do wish I could talk to you of love, Timothea.

TIMOTHEA. You do fine, Colm.

COLM. Like the others you've known.

TIMOTHEA. There haven't been that many.

COLM. Like your husband. He talked love to you, didn't he?

TIMOTHEA. Turn the lock on the door, please.

COLM. You never answer me right off, do you? I noticed that. (*He turns the lock.*)

TIMOTHEA. Yes, Colm. I suppose he sort of talked to

me that way. Eric was a real smarty, good with the words.

COLM. And still is!
Well, if he calls on you again, I'll mark him for life.

TIMOTHEA. You'd do that, wouldn't you?

COLM. I swear it by my arm.

TIMOTHEA. Don't be vexed at him, Colm, tis a thing of nothing.

COLM. Still, it's something you should hear once in a while. Be soothing to you.

TIMOTHEA. It's grand but there's nothin' at the back of it.
It's like a wee kiss behind the ear, nothing more.

COLM. I never once did that!

TIMOTHEA. Ah, Colm, that's not the point.
I'm saying tis a thing of nothing and people only do it when they're trifling with each other.

COLM. We don't trifle with each other!

TIMOTHEA. Get away; we're past all that.

COLM. But we don't, do we. And we never did.

TIMOTHEA. You're a direct man. You get at the purpose of things.

COLM. Would you have me any other way?

TIMOTHEA. I wouldn't change your way and that's the truth. It's your very Irishness I love.

COLM. Pardon?

TIMOTHEA. The sadness in you even when you laugh.
And that sadness is there when you tell me you love me.

COLM. That's happiness.

TIMOTHEA. Well it's a sad happiness.

COLM. That's the Irish?

TIMOTHEA. Aye, the Irish. You have more joy in a wink and a wave than all the men in Liverpool.
Anyway, it isn't the place, is it, it's the man.

COLM. And who do you love?

TIMOTHEA. Who else? Only yourself.

And who do you love?

COLM. Who else? Only yourself.

TIMOTHEA. (*Touched.*) Ah, Colm.

COLM. You see! You do like love talk!
Well, I could say all manner of things to you.
I could liken you to all the things I know.
I could liken you to my curragh. I could say your scuppers are clean. And you're lean without being touchy, so you come through the waves straight and dry.

TIMOTHEA. Smarty.

COLM. I could say you were like sea birds.
Well, no, they do eat fish heads and then go to the toilet in the air.

TIMOTHEA. Oh, bedad!

COLM. Bedad is it? When was it I last heard *bedad*? You've been the Welsh girl since we came home tonight—shed all your lady manners—and I love you better for it.

TIMOTHEA. (*Embarrassed.*) No one could ever understand me around here when I talked it.

COLM. Except me.

TIMOTHEA. Well, isn't it grand about the Wednesday Afternoon Club?

COLM. I'll be shaking, but I'll tell those old ladies all they want to hear. There's a lot, you know.

TIMOTHEA. They're not all old ladies. I'll be there.

COLM. Will you help me pick out what I am to read and what I say? (TIMOTHEA *nods.*) I wouldn't speak the bilge that promotion man wants. It would have to be me that's talkin'.

TIMOTHEA. I can hardly believe that if all goes well, he'll take you down to London and try to get you on the Billy Bright Show.

COLM. Tis never!

TIMOTHEA. Tis!

COLM. I'm not the only Cliffhorn man has never been to London. Where I live, if you get as far as Bunratty they call you a globetrotter.

TIMOTHEA. (*With a sigh.*) London.

COLM. Aye.
Have you been?

TIMOTHEA. For a day and a night. It looked grand.

COLM. If he gets me on the tely, what is it I'm supposed to do?

TIMOTHEA. Well, Billy Bright will introduce you and he'll sit you down beside him and he'll ask you some questions—you know—about the Heads. Then he'll say very casually, "And now, Colm, why don't you read us one or two of your poems?"

COLM. That's when I'll fill me trousers.

TIMOTHEA. You'll get up and walk over to a corner that's got fishnets hung around and sit down in a make-believe boat. You'll reach into your pocket for your book—

COLM. It won't be there!

TIMOTHEA. And you'll read—"This is my country, the sea country.
This is my home, where the fields run deep.
And if there are hills, they are my hills of sea.

COLM. You know it word for word. Why don't *you* read it for me?

TIMOTHEA. After that everyone will applaud you. Billy'll pop over to you and shake you hand and then he'll lead you away.
He'll pay you 50 pounds or more.

COLM. He'll hand it over to me right there?

TIMOTHEA. No, no, no, they'll send it along later.

COLM. I might like this poetry touch.

TIMOTHEA. (*Welsh.*) And they gives you a piece of

money for your trouble.

COLM. Aye.

TIMOTHEA. What was that you were ravin' to Mr. Blackstone about going back to the Heads.

COLM. Well, I *will*, you know, go back one day.

TIMOTHEA. Ah, you will?

COLM. I cannot turn my back on my place. How can I?
I mean it's my—well, what is it my?

TIMOTHEA. You cannot say it's your place anymore. It's the place you once were from. The way I was once from Wales.

COLM. You're always going to be from Wales, you're a Welsh girl. Are you never going back?

TIMOTHEA. Not a drop of it. A young woman is supposed to have better things to do in life than sew the roof, mend the wall, get the milk out of the cow, birth the donkey. I've seen the last of it.

COLM. There's a draw there. There's a beauty.

TIMOTHEA. Maybe there is for you, my dear man, but I know the killing roughness of it as well. I too come from that roughness and I'm not going back to it.
There's a great fear in me of living again where things taste good only because they're hard to come by.

COLM. Well, I must go back to mine. My father's alive, God be good to him, and he's doing the work for the both of us right now.

TIMOTHEA. I'm sure I'm weaker than you are, Colm. I could never leave here.
Yes, I know there's a draw to go back there for you. But it's something I don't ever want to give in to. Can you understand that?

COLM. That Liverpool is a better life?

TIMOTHEA. Yes! I think it is. In Liverpool I don't ever

have to crack ice to make me a basin of water.
I've been to your Heads. It seemed I was always walking uphill.
I never stopped hearing the wind.
And there was the sea, always.

COLM. You won't be coming with me.

TIMOTHEA. I couldn't.
I wondered about it how many times these last weeks.

COLM. I too.

TIMOTHEA. If I'd just been up from Wales, a green girl again, I'd turn around in a minute and be gone with you. Now, I do have my place here and my position. I have a need to rise.

COLM. Well, there's my place, and that's *my* position, and I don't remember when I didn't fish.

TIMOTHEA. Don't go back.

COLM. I must go to the mackerel with my father when it's weather. (*Quick aside.*) Please-God-they'll-be-running.

TIMOTHEA. You'll go back and stay on.

COLM. I would never.

TIMOTHEA. But last night I dreamt you did.

COLM. Come to bed, tis a thing of nothin'. I'm like the priest who can't refuse a call.

TIMOTHEA. But I did dream it. It was like true. You said "ta" and walked out of here. And were gone forever.

COLM. I wouldn't stay on. There's been an empty space beside me in bed for so much of my life—now that it's gone—(*He doesn't finish his thought.*)

TIMOTHEA. I haven't been with you for so much of my life, that if you left me now, I don't know what.

COLM. Don't be afraid of your dreams. Last night I dreamt we were out on the water and in lightning. Our bed became my curragh, and these were the gunwhales, and the window, which was being cooled by the moon, was our sail. We were riding through waves with a load of fish so big but it was sinking us.

TIMOTHEA. And who was I in your dream, the MacAfee?

COLM. You were you.
I keep dreaming about the sea, and it's come to me in the time I was here that I love it.
Well, no man should die until he's loved one thing.

TIMOTHEA. And now he loves two.

COLM. Aye.

TIMOTHEA. I don't know who you are at all, tonight, Colm.

COLM. Come to bed! Sail in our curragh to your dreams.
Give me your hands and I'll hold them warm. Let your hair surround us so we lose our place.
In the morning, tell me your dreams, if you remember dreams, and if I can, I'll unravel them.

TIMOTHEA. Smarty.

(*Lights dim to black.*)

END OF SCENE 2

ACT TWO

SCENE 3

Midday. TIMOTHEA *is alone onstage, dressed smartly for the ladies club. She is agitated, nervously talking into the new and gleaming black telephone installed on the table stage center. Her voice is the only one heard.*

TIMOTHEA. I don't *know* where he is.
(*What'll I tell Mr. Blackstone?*)
Tell Mr. Blackstone whatever you feel like. No: Tell him he's on his way home. And he'll be there.
(*I'm going to get the sack for this.*)
You won't get the sack.
(*Hasn't he ever stood up in front—*)
Well, naturally he's never stood up in front of a group of strangers. There are no strangers where he comes from. But it's more than that.
(*Doesn't he want to go down to London?*)
No, no, no. Of course I want us to go to London.
(*Right. Well what'll I tell the boss?*)
Just tell him we won't need to cancel.
(*What happens when he doesn't show?*)
I don't know what I'll do. (TIMOTHEA *is in tears.*)
(*Alright, alright. I'll pick you up. Be right over.*)
Grand. It's the top floor. Buzz the buzzer.
(*Goodbye.*)
Goodbye.

(TIMOTHEA *holds the disconnected receiver for a moment then sets it down. She straightens her suit nervously in the mirror. Abruptly the telephone rings. She thinks it might be* COLM *but it is Mr. Blackstone, whose voice is never heard.*

TIMOTHEA. Hello?
(*How do you do, Miss Stiles. Has Mr. Howard been onto you yet?*
Yes, sir. I've just been talking to him.
(*Well, you see our problem; where is our poet?*)
I have no idea.
(*You realize the importance of this day for him as well as us, don't you?*)

Yes sir, I know how important it is.
(*That it is vital to the selling of our book?*)
Vital.
(*Incalculable.*)
Incalculable.
(*He was out when you came home?*)
Found him gone.
(*Is he that scared of speaking in public?*)
Nervous, yes sir, not *scared.*
(*We cannot continue this project if he is not responsible for himself.*)
He will be there, sir.
(*At what time?*)
Two o'clock.
(*Did you call your pub?*)
He wouldn't be at the pub now, sir, not in the middle of the day.
(*Where could he have gone?*)
Just—gone for a walk—such a grand day.
(*I do hope your new telephone is working satisfactoraly.*)
It is an excellent telephone and thank you for having it installed for us.

(COLM *has been heard offstage, singing up the stairs.*)

TIMOTHEA. He will be there, Mr. Blackstone. I give you my word. Goodbye, sir.
(*Goodbye Miss Stiles.*)
(TIMOTHEA *hangs up the telephone.*)

(COLM *enters, bruised, flying, unshaven, soiled, singing. This song, "Foggy Dew,"—the Irish protest song—is sung to the same tune as the drinking song in Act II Scene 1, but here it is a handsome song and*

COLM *sings it with a purity come from love for its words. He finishes the song or sings as much as* TIMOTHEA *will allow.*

COLM. Right proudly high over Dublin town
They hung out a flag of war
'Twas better to die 'neath an Irish sky
Oh, see the new black te-le-phone
And from the plains of Cliffhorn Heads
Strong men came harrying through
While Britannia's sons with their long range guns
Sailed in from the foggy dew.
(*Before* TIMOTHEA *can say anything or because she doesn't,* COLM *speaks. There's a dreadful edge to his voice.*) I killed me a power of whiskey today. A power of whiskey. (COLM *goes to the kitchen and fetches himself a bottle of stout.*) I wonder if there's anyone here can sing us a song?

(TIMOTHEA *neatly grabs the bottle and smashes it in the kitchen sink.*)

COLM. Now don't go gettin' ratty.
TIMOTHEA. Don't you go gettin' ratty, Colm boyo—do you know what day it is?
COLM. It is a Wednesday.
TIMOTHEA. You could do with a wash.
COLM. Ah.
TIMOTHEA. You could do with a shave as well.
COLM. And why would that be?
TIMOTHEA. Now don't go tellin' us it slipped your mind.
COLM. It didn't slip me mind. It changed me mind.
TIMOTHEA. I think you've got a slate loose.
COLM. Did you read the newspaper?
TIMOTHEA. Yes.
COLM. About—

TIMOTHEA. I read it, Colm.

COLM. Where it says that Mr. Blackstone found me under a mushroom—like I was one of the "little people?" And where it says that I'm the "Jack Frost of the Irish sea?"

TIMOTHEA. Robert.

COLM. Robert.
And naturally it says I'm primitive once again.
Well don't confuse primitive with stupid. It's not the same thing at-all at-all.

TIMOTHEA. Wear your new trousers, Colm.

COLM. "Wear your new trousers, Colm"—you're not getting what I'm telling you. I'm not going there to be made a bigger fool than I already am. Bigger primitive.

TIMOTHEA. You've got to do it.

COLM. Got to do it?

TIMOTHEA. Yes. Got to do it. What harm is there in reading a few words? (TIMOTHEA *has changed, she seems on the verge of tears.*)

COLM. It's that important to you, readin' the words.

TIMOTHEA. Important for us.

COLM. Important for you.

TIMOTHEA. I want it for us.

COLM. Words is nothing.

TIMOTHEA. (TIMOTHEA'S *tension bursts.*) Words is everything to us! It's all I had of you for a year-and-a-half, two winters and a summer of not knowing who it was behind the words, but knowing that a feeling in me was something I'd never known in my life. Wondering what it was—and how could it be love, if it was only words? There's no such thing—I thought. I didn't know what was there in the words that made me turn around and go to Maggie's wedding at the Heads. But when I saw you out back of the church, I knew. You're the boy. All of him you. And that was it.
There's nothing that's come of my life here—my mar-

riage—none of it—that's meant so much.
And it was all in your words and it was all true.

(COLM *goes to* TIMOTHEA *and hugs her and begins to weep without control. Or he might just sit, stone sober, staring away from her. Or he might choose some other action.*)

TIMOTHEA. What is it?

(COLM *reveals a worn letter and envelope he's been carrying around. He might re-read it to himself. Or ball it up and throw it. Or merely drop it.*)

TIMOTHEA. God, what is it? Please, Colm, tell me.

(*Dulled by the shock of the words in the letter, he's reduced to simplicity.*)

COLM. A letter came for me in the post this morning.
TIMOTHEA. What does it say?
COLM. Words.
TIMOTHEA. Tell me, please.
COLM. It's from Mrs. Stoney. (*He pauses.*) They found the MacAfee.
TIMOTHEA. Oh, Colm.
COLM. He'd been 10 days gone.
He'd been dead. In the water. For 10 days. (*He pauses.*) There was no way of knowing it was the MacAfee except by his jersey. (*To himself.*) I wish they hadn't found him like that—I never want to be found like that by any man.
TIMOTHEA. You're not going to drown.
COLM. No, I'm not—not here. I'm safe here, am't I?

(*Pause.*) The thing of it was, you see, he came into Cliffhorn Heads only to be buried again. (*He pauses.*) He was a great rower and a great fisher—(*Quickly.*) God-be-good-to-him—he could haul with any one of us. The softest part of him was his teeth.
I cannot understand his drowning!

TIMOTHEA. All things go their proper length, Colm. Maybe the MacAfee was gone to his.

COLM. It was me killed him. (*A moment passes.*)

TIMOTHEA. You don't kill a man by letting him be.

COLM. No, I killed the man I rowed with all these years. (*To himself.*) A-ah, my good father gone dark! (*The door buzzer buzzes once and then again.*)

TIMOTHEA. When is the funeral to be?

COLM. Yesterday. (*The buzzer buzzes. The lights dim more slowly to black.*)

END OF SCENE 3

ACT TWO

SCENE 4

The curtain is drawn. Or the stage is dark, if there is no curtain. COLM, *unshaven, dressed as he was in the previous scene, crosses to a spotlit lectern downstage. He speaks to the audience indirectly, not as though they were members of the Wednesday Afternoon Club.*

COLM. I'll say a few words to you and then read you some marks that I made at a place as far away from this room as the other side of life. An island by the name of Cliffhorn Heads. In my language, the Irish, it would be called "Inish Shinderra." (*He pauses.*) Do any of you remember what a sunrise is like?

Sort of a gray meeting of the clouds at the east, and then a lightening of the sky, swiftening, lightening, swiftening, lightening until it is there?

Have any of you ever been out on the dark water, with not much sea running, and have known, really for true, that in a bit you'd be able to hold your hands out like this (*He holds his arms straight out at eye level, fingers stretched and raises them slightly.*) so that they could be warmed by the sun that is coming? For these elegances, you must become a fisherman. (*He pauses.*)

Fishing is, after all, a simple matter. You set your nets and you haul them in. You stay off the rocks at night and you anchor with care. And you look for signs that the sky is kind enough to provide. (*He pauses.*)

There are a number of people who do not understand the sea and I am among them. The sea is never simple – with its currents and strange habits – and bears watching. The sea is not a sentimental place to go – it is waiting for you to make a mistake. After all my years on it, I am kin to it, but I am not married to it – the sea is not a woman, after all. (*He pauses.*)

My partner is called the MacAfee.

From the time I could walk, I remember he had white hair, and a pipe growing out of his mouth. He'd smoke anything – I imagined – cow dung – just to keep his face lit. (*Pause.*)

There was never a man I loved more than the MacAfee. Men liked him every way there was to like a man. Ah, the eyes on him, like two candles burning. In one stroke of his eyes he could give you all the love you needed to last you a year. (*Pause.*)

I recall three ways I saw him.
The one was standing in the curragh, knee high in haddock—the first boat to fill—the hairs on his beard shiny from fish slime. And him calling out to me, just calling out to me.
The second, I see him at the Captain's with a black pint in front of him and another in his hand, drinking with us in front of the fire, older than us and smarter, too, but never letting on unless it was needed.
I see him then at Sunday breakfast. It would have been a crab or two with a thick buttered bannock and a pint. He was a grand man. You should have known him.
Anyhow, there's an old fisherman drowned who'll live in me forever. (*Without meaning to,* COLM *has begun to see the MacAfee. Now, suddenly, he has put himself in the curragh with the MacAfee at the time of his drowning. Whatever* COLM *feels about it can be seen and heard in* COLM'S *momentary insanity.*)
When we would go to fish, we might carry a small sail on the curragh and set it right. Now if the seas were running high and the wind turning in sudden gusts, it would send us over the wave, and out, and down, into the vale between the waves. And my heart went down there, and my soul went along, too, if I had a soul at the time.
Oh, I knew we'd rise again, but it always seemed like tomorrow when we came above the wave, and then it was higher than before.
And we'd perch on the new wave a moment, the gale holding us balanced longer than ever, and then AAAAAAAAAAAAAAAAAAAAAAAH—it was OUT and DOWN and into that dark place between the waves that want to hold you there. That place where the wind does not go. And again you be up, high, balanced. And then OUT and DOWN. All over again. (COLM *pauses a moment, stabilizing himself, relieved.*)

After a while of this, and when it looks like you might get home again and walk along a boreen, or duck under a laundry line, you begin to feel strong. And even though the wind is trying to tear your clothes away, you don't mind. You're grinning, and the wind is hissing in your ears, and you're sailing home!
But you should never feel as though you've conquered the sea. If you do, there's any number of words for the sort of fool you are. And the sea doesn't ever weary of making fools of us. For if it sends us home at night to light our fires, it's only because it wants us back to sport with us another time.
Don't ever think you had anything to do with it. Because you'll be mistaken.
Or maybe not. (*Pause.*)
When I was young, a wave so high swept across the low waist of our island and left the islandmen trembling with fear, and me among them. I will always have that fear, but am now strong enough to visit the sea and live on it a while.
It has been my life good and bad.
And the sea provides.
The sea provides. (*Pause.*)
The oldies knit these pretty jerseys for us. The widows. They keen their yarn and knit this pattern into each one of them. Every town along both coasts has its own pattern and this is ours.
Would you like to know why they knit our jerseys at night? The sheep are asleep at night, and are content. They think the jerseys will be better for it. And so be the men inside them. (*Pause.*)
Now when a man floats into our harbor and the fish have taken out his eyes and nibbled off his lips, we can

tell from his jersey where he might have come to us from. And so he gets brought home.
But the cleanest burial is when you slip away and are gone.
You should never be found by another man. You should make sure you go deep and not ever rise to the surface.
Let the people remember you the way you were the morning you went out.
You shouldn't go floating down the coast looking for your harbor while the fish eat from you for days and wash up on the shore like that, putting frights into people and asking to be buried again, this time in the ground.
Anyhow; that's why we wear these very pretty jerseys. They settle the question of dress six days out of seven. But I was going to read you sonnets, wasn't I?, from this idiot book. I was going to tell you that the sea was a single great arm holding us all in our place, or some such nonsense. Instead, I'll tell you a short one.

We are now weavers, we are now caulkers
We are now baiters, we are now young.

We are now rowers, we are now fishers
We are now masters, we are now men.

We are now drinkers, we are now singers,
We are now mourners, we are now dead.

(*The lights fade to black.* COLM *does not move from the lectern.*)

END OF SCENE 4

ACT TWO

Scene 5

Without stopping the action, the lights cross fade or the curtain opens. TIMOTHEA *is discovered in a special light, seated at the foot of her bed, reading a letter.*

TIMOTHEA. "Dear Love—I've had my hands full for a week now building the new curragh. If I keep at it, it'll be afloat for the spring runs.
You know—I found a dog hanging around the house? No one seems to care where he might have come to me from, but on he stays. Smiggy guessed he fell overboard off the Russian trawler in the storm and swam ashore. He's a brave lump of a dog and has a lively enough step, but the heaviest of his work is in going out and then coming back in. Do you think I could ever teach him to kick the door shut after him? (*A special has come up to half to reveal* COLM *standing, maybe in the doorway of his house, looking down.*)
I'll be writing you after the curragh's in. I think that would be a good thing. If you can, would *you* write and say what you are doing?
So, goodnight. I think about you every minute of the day and night. I'm sort of crying now and I think you are, too. As ever, Colm." (TIMOTHEA *crosses to the table and sits, takes out a piece of paper. She holds her pen above the page before she begins, carefully, to write. She speaks slowly.*) My dearest, Colm—

CURTAIN

The Sea: The sea faces Colm (I,1) and certainly imprisons him. He feels this, but it isn't until Act II that he defines his feelings for it. In a lesser way, it would be as if a New Yorker who rode the subway every day of his life left the city and lived without subways and so began to miss the subway; the push, the action, the smell, the danger, the secret romance, even the fear. To Colm, the sea is a place he has to be to live, always changing yet always the same. That is; the sea is always inventing moods to challenge, mystify or to be admired, as well as always being the dependable place to go for food, and always dangerous. The sea is a character in the play, certainly as much as the MacAfee is a character in it, and in a two-character play, you need all the friends you can get.

The Sky: If the proscenium is high (as it was at the Eisenhower Theater, Kennedy Center) and the design more elaborate (as it was at the Portland Stage Company)—the sky can become important to the production. Seen at all times above the interior set of Timothea's top-storey flat, can be the sky. And the outlines of the Georgian finials show against the sky, both day and night; fair or foul.

Wardrobe: Colm's style of dress undergoes a serious change; Timothea tries to make him over into a trendier piece of work. From his wool trousers (trousers that can stand alone, without a tenant) he progresses to whatever Timothea would consider more stylish. Timothea's change is subtler, and ought to be taken more from her character seen falling in love. We see her become aware and care more about her "look."

The Set: The set is not as important as the illusion of a set and "Sea Marks" has been produced with the barest representation of a set (Manhattan Theatre Club). At the other extreme, the set at the Center Theatre in Hollywood was so realistic and solidly built that an aged couple from New Jersey asked if they might live in it between performances. (We could not agree on rent.) Colm's house unit (I,1) revolved to become Timothea's kitchen (I,3) and the church wall above the graveyard (I,2) opened up to become the central part of Timothea's flat (I,3). "Sea Marks" has even been presented in-the-round; though I feel the round's unique possibilities are squandered on theater and ought only to be bestowed on sports—hockey, boxing, basketball—where its full impact can be enjoyed.

If the theater has an unusually small stage, as did the Players Theatre (New York), without the usual exits or adequate height, the chance for illusion is nearly lost. Ingenious devices were used, such as three sets of vertical panels painted with abstractions of seascape and, when revolved, cityscape of Liverpool; but were braver than they were successful.

As long as the action is allowed to flow across the stage, that is, the front door is opposite the kitchen, for example, the bath is equi-distant; scenes can have natural movement. As long as the lighting of the stage is not spiritless; and the playing areas; hearth, bed, window, table, are lit by focused instruments, the set can change and the actors will be given a fair chance to perform the play.

Dialects: Occasionally, Timothea lapses into a strong, Welsh country accent; rich, rhythmic sounds coming from vaguely the same Celtic origins as Colm's Irish. It is unique; it has the same music as Colm's, but a more demanding tone to it, more exclamation points. Except for her brief regressions, her accent in the main body of the play is citified English. To what extent, only the ear of the director will know. She should not, I suggest, sound like a member of Burke's Peerage, as if she worked for Harrod's in London and had taken on certain colors of her clients. She works in Liverpool, to her mind "only halfway to London." Colm's dialect is the calm, songing accent of the west. It is a passive sound; no Dublin tensions here, just a swelling of the language that lends itself to free verse or easy quietude. It is the difference between Waterville (Maine) and New York, or the difference between Teruel and Madrid.

I've seen Colm played without an Irish accent of any kind at the Actors Theatre in Louisville—the character was more a mountain Colm than a sea Colm; but the labor was in him, and Colm is a laborer, not a yachtsman. I was put off at first, but the Yin and Yang between the characters was there and as I grew accustomed to the freshness of it I didn't miss the accent at all. Overall: less is more. These accents, fully done, might act as a soporific to certain audiences.

Ages: Colm can be played realistically between the

ages of 35 and 65. Loneliness, or aloneness, is not exclusive. Timothea should not be younger than her late 20's. Her age should rise proportionately to his, or his to hers, but not above her mid-fifties.

Sound and Music: When the theater doors are opened and the audience is being seated there should be a series of uncomplicated melodies played on penny-whistle and celtic harp, as bright as need be, to enhance the simplicity of the opening scene. Moments before the "curtain is raised" the music should dissolve into a measured crashing of the surf; not the drama of storm surf. Theater music can be used, of course, between the acts or noticeably long scene changes. Sound effects of sea or traffic or ship travel can be taped without risk of copyright infringement from sound effect records published specifically for these uses. Permission to use music from published albums is another matter and should be gotten from the music publisher whose name appears on each specific album.

Music has been been well used within the play. During the opening letters and in act I scene 5 when Timothea is going back over her first experience with a man.

Music can be found, traditional Irish airs, pub songs, reels on: 1) Albums Five and Seven of the Chieftains, 2) Derek Bell's "Carolon's Receipt" album, 3) the soundtrack album for "Barry Lyndon," 4) The Clancy Brothers' "The Rising of the Moon" album, 5) the Bothy Band albums. Rights for usage should be gotten in writing from the music publishers named on the album.

Pronunciations and Meanings: Certain words are obvious to some, obscure to others. At the suggestion of the Artistic Director of the Florida Studio Theatre, I'll presume to list a few. *Colm* is pronounced "column" or can be rounded off to rhyme with "holme," sounding the "l" slightly rather than as "comb." *MacAfee* is a Scots name and is pronounced here "mac-ah-fee," all syllables equal. *Glamorganshire*, home of the Morgans is "gluh-morgan-shur." *Gunwhales* is "gunnels." *Minott* is simply "min-ott." *Liam* is "lee-um." *Potcheen* (actually spelled "poteen") is a clear fluid, secretly brewed, and casually referred to as "whiskey." "Potcheen" may be substituted for the word "whiskey" and is pronounced "pot-cheen." *Curragh* is pronounced here either "coor-ah" or "cur-ug." These are smart looking boats, all of them black, made of canvas stretched over a wood frame. They are surprisingly light for their length (16 to 18 feet) and so have the ability to be tossed high and avoid the aggravations of the wave, endured by heavier hulls, say, of doryboats that sit deeply in the water. A curragh has a round bottom, a flat transom, an upturned prow and is propelled by bladeless oars. As if all this wasn't enough, some carry a vial of holy water lashed to the stem. *Inish Shinderra* means nothing coherent, really, but comes from Colm's imagination. An "inish" is an island, and "shinderra" means "it is finished," as a meal is finished or, in Colm's case, something more. A *gob* is a mouth, a *yob* is an idiot. A *bannock* is bread baked into a roll. *Bedad* is an expletive, maybe derived from "be dead!" A *set* is a noun taken from the verb "to set" nets. *A woman to cut the toes off a man*, means that she's a woman to confine a man. A *boreen* is a lane.

Thesis: If this play is about anything, it might be about knowing our place. Especially in liquid times, when we can easily flow wherever, and seemingly become whatever.

To hold a way of life, something secretly treasured, maybe without knowing it, has become an obsolete idea, now called stagnation. But being mobile, trading up, "bettering yourself" is a respectable life's work, while other, simpler concerns are postponed.

—Gardner McKay

SEA MARKS PROP PLOT

Preset props — Timothea's unit

soup cup with spoon and water — L. on mantlepiece
 on coaster
Letters from Colm — tucked in between books R. on
 mantel
 — tucked in between books L. on
 mantel
 — 2 on top of writing paper on
 floor US of window seat
 — on hearth on top of writing paper
book, writing paper, pen — on hearth
 — on floor US of window seat
scotch tape or pushpins on mantel
large pillow — C. on bed
2 small pillows — C. on bed
alarm clock — on bed table set at 11:30
rushes — in vase on plant stand, R. of bed
2 books — on floor L. of window seat
afghan — on ottoman

Preset in kitchen

empty incense holder — kitchen counter
matches — kitchen counter
corkscrew — kitchen counter
scotch glass — kitchen counter
2 wine glasses — kitchen
2nd dinner set-up — kitchen counter (2 plates, 2 forks,
 2 spoons, 2 knives, 2 napkins, 2 placemats)
1st dinner set-up — on round table (2 plates, 2 forks,

2 spoons, 2 knives, 2 napkins, 2 water glasses with little water in them, candlestick, stew dish with ladle, ashtray, plates are dirty, all of the above are on a tablecloth which is supported by a piece of wood cut to fit the dinner table)

Preset props — Colm's unit

pipe, tobacco, matches — on table R.
ashtray — on table R. full
writing paper, pencil — on table, C.
Timothea's letter #2 — under writing paper
champerpot — under washstand R.

Preset props on prop table

Tim's purse with wrapped Sea Sonnets in side
hairbrush
Colm's #1 letter
string bag with crab, potatoes, full wine bottle, corked, English muffins, capped full Guinness bottle
6 empty stout bottles in carrying case
canvas bag with threaded needle
sewing bag with thread and knife
2 sets of keys

Preset props — in R. wing

bench
nearly full corked whiskey bottle
tin suitcase

Preset props — in dressing room

Tim's hat and gloves

punch cup with a little punch liquid
stout bottle — on Colm's table
Tim's letter #1 — in Colm's hat
pen box, wrapped — in Colm's right breast pocket

Preset furniture — Timothea's unit

bed — UC
table with lamp — L. of bed
screen — U of bed table
trunk — D. of bed
rug — under and D. of bed
— D. of hearth
ottoman — DL of mantle (with pillow on it)
plant stand — UR of bed with vase on it
doormat — at entrance doorway
umbrella stand — DR of entrance platform
bric a brac — R. of mantle
fireplace — UL
windowseat — DL
large round table — UR of window seat
chair — U of table (with pillow on it)
rocker — DR of bed
quilt — on trunk

Preset furniture — Colm's unit

square table — C
chair — U of table
washstand — UR

I,1 Strike

washstand, table, chair from Colm's unit to R. wing
Colm's unit pulled back
Tim's coat and scarf to changing area

letters, writing paper, pens from Tim's unit
spoon and mug
books to L. on floor by windowseat
pipe, matches and tobacco to dressing room
Colm's slicker, hat and boots

I,2 prop preset
bench—CL on platform
whiskey bench—under bench

I,2 Strike

bench
wrapping and string
pen case to mantle
bottle and cup struck by actors

I,3 prop preset

tin suitcase—SR
dinner set-up #1—to round table
pipe, matches tobacco—to Colm's suit jacket pocket
Colm's suit jacket—to peg on Tim's door
ashtray—on mantle
pen case—on mantle
I,3—nothing struck
I,4—nothing preset or struck
I,5—nothing preset

I,5 Strike

Colm's clothes
dinner set-up to kitchen
candle to kitchen counter

I,6 prop preset

6 empty stout bottles to round table
bed made, pillows set
sewing bag carried to tin suitcase by Colm
Colm's cap

—Compiled by Tom W. Picard

ITEM-BY-ITEM COSTUME LIST

Colm	*Timothea*
sea gear:	slip
sea pants	loafers
black rubber sea boots	heeled shoes
sou'wester	bedroom slippers
oilskin	trench coat
cotton union suit	cardigan
ragg socks	blouse
fisherman sweater (2)	wool skirt
wool cap	shirtwaist dress
black jacket	pullover
wool pants	slacks
white oxfordcloth shirt	nightgown
dark old-fashioned tie	robe
hightop black shoes	pullover with collar
handkerchief	blouse
wool vest	skirt
suspenders	dress
sweatshirt	wool suit
pants	blouse with bow
belt	hat (2?)
watch	scarf (4?)
shoes (new)	knee socks (2)
socks	watch
	chain with religious medal
	earrings
	crocheted gloves
	socks
	jewelry (II,2)

ROUGH COSTUME PLOT

COLM

ACT I

Scene 1

union suit (cotton—long sleeve/short leg—top only visible)
sea pants with suspenders
heavy ragg socks
add:
fisherman sweater
oilskin
sou'wester
black rubber sea boots
(In scene must change into and out of sea gear and get wet)
(CHANGE ---- pants, sweater)

Scene 2

wool cap
tweed jacket
white oxfordcloth shirt
dark tie
wool pants
hightop black shoes
handkerchief
(Loses cap in scene, changes tie)
(CHANGE---- jacket, shirt, tie)

ROUGH COSTUME PLOT

Scene 3

wool vest
same fisherman sweater
same pants
same socks
same shoes
(Loses vest)
(CHANGE – – – – lose sweater, pants, shoes)

Scene 4

same union suit
same socks
(Uses her robe)

Scene 5

No change

Scene 6

same wool pants
suspenders
same socks
same underwear (top visible)

ACT II

Scene 1

sweatshirt
corduroy pants

belt
watch
sweater double
same socks
(Changes from sweatshirt to sweater double in scene—
might have normal t-shirt on at this point)

Scene 2

(add:) new socks
same wool cap
same suit jacket

Scene 3

changes pants—old pants
same fisherman sweater double
same wool cap
old wool slacks (from ACT I)
same Clarke's shoes
same socks (from Act II, scene 2)
(MAY need prop pants and shirt in scene.)
(loses jacket and cap)

Scene 4

No change
(CHANGE ---- pants, shoes)

Scene 5

same sea pants
same ragg socks
same fisherman sweater

ROUGH COSTUME PLOT

TIMOTHEA

ACT I

Scene 1

hat
trench coat
scarf
cardigan sweater
blouse
wool skirt
knee socks
pantyhose
loafers
watch
chain with religious medal
slip
bra
(During scene loses hat, scarf, coat sweater)
(CHANGE – – – – out of blouse, skirt, kneesocks, loafers)

Scene 2

shirtwaist dress
scarf
heeled shoes
earrings
crocheted gloves
hat

same slip and pantyhose
(CHANGE - - - - out of dress, shoes, scarf, slip)

Scene 3

pullover
slacks
socks
same bra
(During scene she loses pullover, slacks, socks, bra)
nightgown
robe

Scene 4

same robe

Scene 5

same robe

Scene 6

same bra
pullover with collar
same wool skirt
same loafers
same trenchcoat
scarf
kneesocks (different color)

ACT II

Scene 1

scarf (worn like babushka)
trench coat

cardigan
blouse (prettier than the first)
skirt (a new one)
loafers
bra
hose
socks
(During scene loses scarf and trench coat and cardigan)
(CHANGE - - - - loses blouse, skirt, socks, shoes)

Scene 2

Party dress
jewelry
same shoes with heels
trenchcoat

Scene 3

telephone
wool suit
blouse with bow
same heeled shoes
same bra
same hose
same slip

Scene 5

Doesn't appear

Scene 6

same slip
same robe
slippers

FOGGY DEW

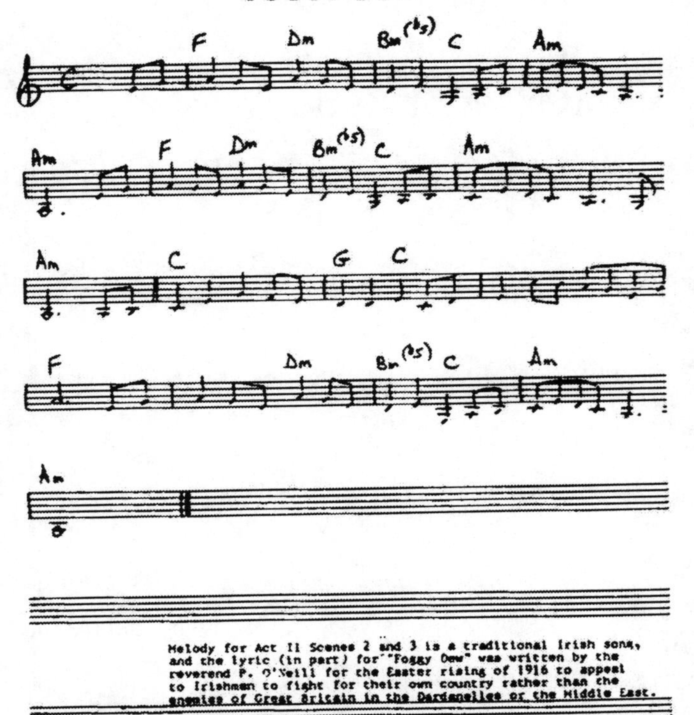
F Dm Bm(b5) C Am
Am F Dm Bm(b5) C Am
Am C G C
F Dm Bm(b5) C Am
Am
Melody for Act II Scenes 2 and 3 is a traditional Irish song, and the lyric (in part) for "Foggy Dew" was written by the reverend P. O'Neill for the Easter rising of 1916 to appeal to Irishmen to fight for their own country rather than the enemies of Great Britain in the Dardanelles or the Middle East.

Also By

Gardner McKay

In Order of Appearance

Masters of the Sea

Toyer

Untold Damage

OTHER TITLES AVAILABLE FROM SAMUEL FRENCH

PERFECT WEDDING
Robin Hawdon

Comedy / 2m, 4f / Interior

A man wakes up in the bridal suite on his wedding morning to find an extremely attractive naked girl in bed beside him. In the depths of a stag night hangover, he can't even remember meeting her. Before he can get her out, his bride to be arrives to dress for the wedding. In the ensuing panic, the girl is locked in the bathroom. The best man is persuaded to claim her, but he gets confused and introduces the chamber maid to the bride as his date. The crisis escalates to nuclear levels by the time the mother of the bride and the best man's actual girlfriend arrive. This rare combination of riotous farce and touching love story has provoked waves of laughter across Europe and America.

"Laughs abound."
– *Wisconsin Advocate*

"The full house audience roared with delight."
– *Green Bay Gazette*

SAMUELFRENCH.COM

OTHER TITLES AVAILABLE FROM SAMUEL FRENCH

VERONICA'S ROOM
Ira Levin

Thriller / 2m, 2f / Interior

This chilling mystery thriller by the author of *Rosemary's Baby* explores the thin line between fantasy and reality, madness and murder. Students Susan and Larry find themselves as guests enticed to the Brabissant mansion by its dissolute caretakers, the lonely Mackeys. Struck by Susan's strong resemblance to Veronica Brabissant, long-dead daughter of the family for whom they work, the older couple gradually induce her to impersonate Veronica briefly to solace the only living Brabissant, her addled sister who believes Veronica alive. Once dressed in Veronica's clothes, Susan finds herself locked in the role and locked in Veronica's room. Or is she Veronica, in 1935, pretending to be an imaginary Susan?

"Like being trapped in someone else's nightmare...jarring and (with a) surprising climax...a neat, elegant thriller."
– *Village Voice*